Silvia Vera Laceiras

Digital processing of cytogenetic images for their classification

Silvia Vera Laceiras

Digital processing of cytogenetic images for their classification

According to the comet assay technique for the detection of DNA damage

ScienciaScripts

Summary

This final master's thesis aims to develop a bioinformatics tool to detect DNA nucleoids (with heads and tails) in fluorescence through image recognition, for subsequent classification according to the comet assay technique. The aim is to automate and manage their storage, and to optimise processes in the cytogenetics laboratory.

To this end, possible methods to be applied are evaluated and those combining mathematical algorithms, computational algorithms, neural networks and neuro-fuzzy systems are selected.

The developed method performs detection and segmentation in three steps:

- First: an initial pre-processing and segmentation of the raw image is carried out.
- Second, the fragments obtained are classified by neural networks into three groups: head, tail and bottom.
- Third: heads or cores and tails are measured and re-analysed, sorted according to their ratio.

This process of detection, segmentation and classification was tested using the case study with cytogenetic imaging in a comet assay of the Laboratory of General Cytogenetics and Environmental Monitoring of the Institute of Subtropical Biology UNaM-IBS-CONICET.

The results exposed through the model evaluation gave an Average *Accuracy* (*Accuracy*) 0.92% and harmonic mean (*Fmeasure*) 0.96% were achieved through models combining classification methods using hybrid algorithms, neural networks, neuro-fuzzy system and classification functions.

Keywords: Comet assay, neural networks, neuro-fuzzy algorithms, fuzzy logic, classification algorithms, digital image processing, cytogenetics.

Abstract

The objective of this thesis is the development of a bioinformatics tool that allows to detect DNA nucleoids (with heads and tails) through the recognition of images in fluorescence, for its subsequent classification according to comet assay technique. It is sought to automate and manage their storage, and to optimise processes in the cytogenetic laboratory.

For this purpose, possible methods are evaluated and the ones selected combine mathematical and computer algorithms, neural networks and fuzzy.

The developed method performs detection and segmentation in three steps:

- First: a pre-process and initial segmentation of the raw image is carried out.
- Second: the fragments obtained are classified by means of a convolutional neural network (CNN) into three groups: head, tail and bottom.
- Third: heads or cores and tails are measured, re-analyzed, and classified according to its proportional ratio.

This detection, segmentation and classification process was verified by means of case study with cytogenetic images during the comet assay in General Cytogenetic and Environmental Monitoring Laboratory of Subtropical Biology Institute, UNaM-IBS-CONICET.

The results presented through the evaluation of the model gave accuracy of 0.92 and Fmeasure of 0.96 were models that combine classification methods that make use of hybrid algorithms, neuronal networks, neuro-fuzzy algorithms and classification functions.

Keywords: Comet assay, neural networks, neurofuzzy algorithms, fuzzy logic, classification algorithms, digital image processing, cytogenetics.

Acknowledgements

I would like to thank my thesis supervisors, Dr María Inés Pisarello and Dr Jacqueline Caffetti for their time and for advising me with warmth and precision, sharing their knowledge to achieve a good work.

To the authorities and teachers of the master's degree of the Faculty of Exact, Chemical and Natural Sciences of the UNaM and the Faculty of Exact, Natural Sciences and Surveying of the UNNE who allowed me to improve my knowledge and created this motivation in me.

To my dear people, friends and fellow students who made this journey very pleasant.

To my family who accompanied every step of the way with love and understanding.

And to God for giving me peace and strength to achieve my goals so that this knowledge can be useful to society.

Index

1

Introduction

Introduction

1.1 Context and justification :

The Laboratory of General Cytogenetics and Environmental Monitoring of the Institute of Subtropical Biology at the Faculty of Exact, Chemical and Natural Sciences; National University of Misiones; CONICET (UNAM-IBS-CONICET) analyses genetic damage in aquatic organisms and its impact on human health as a consequence of exposure to urban and industrial pollutants present in rivers and streams in different parts of the Province of Misiones. For these purposes, two specific techniques are currently being used, one is the Comet Assay Test or Single Cell Gel Electrophoresis (SCGE) and the Micronucleus Test.

The test that is being developed and expanded is the Comet Test or gel electrophoresis of individual cells, applied to bioindicator organisms exposed to water samples taken from the Paraná River, in different sections or points of the province.

The analysis and hand-crafted visual classification of the images obtained can become tedious and dependent on the expert geneticist, as well as being susceptible to interpretation biases when more than one researcher is involved in the observation process.

To facilitate the work of the Laboratory, it is proposed to investigate the possibility of applying automatic classification and segmentation techniques to the cytogenetic images obtained by epifluorescence microscopy for the comet assay, and to perform *benchmarking* with the different options.

The General Cytogenetics and Environmental Monitoring Laboratory (UNAM-IBS-CONICET) started its activities in 1989, focusing on cytogenetic-evolutionary studies in different animal models with main emphasis on neotropical freshwater fish. Later, the human cytogenetics line was incorporated, providing diagnostic services under an agreement between the UNaM and the Social Security Institute of the Province of Misiones (IPS). Since 1993, the line of mutagenesis and environmental monitoring has been included, which aims to study the impact of pollutants in natural environments and in laboratory bioassays through cytogenetic-molecular techniques. Currently, the laboratory is made up of its director, Dr. Alberto Fenocchio; teacher-researchers: Dr. Jacqueline Caffetti and Lic. Héctor Roncati; as well as thesis students, graduate and postgraduate scholarship holders: Angemara Rau, Sergio Müller and Mari Florencia Rivero.

The laboratory, in its line of research on aquatic pollutants, applies specific toxicological genetics techniques, such as the Comet Assay.

These so-called "genetic biomarkers" are useful as early warning signals in polluted watercourses, and their analysis is therefore of predictive interest in assessments of watercourse quality status and watershed management.[1].

The comet assay is a technique where 100 cells are counted for each individual (out of a total of 10-15 individuals per treatment). These 100 cells are sorted into 5 classes depending on the fluorescence intensity of the length of the "comet tails". The fluorescence that "stains" the deoxyribonucleic acid (*DNA*) makes it possible to observe the manifestations that are equivalent to the amount of fragmented or damaged *DNA:* class 0 (no damage, i.e. no tail); class 1 (tail size up to one times the diameter of the head); class 2 (tail size up to twice the diameter of the head); class 3 (tail size up to three times the diameter of the head) and class 4 (almost all *DNA* appears fragmented in the tail, in this class are included the abnormal ones with identical characteristics).

The recording and classification of these cell types is done visually and by hand and then recorded manually. Once all cells are sorted into the 5 classes, the *DNA* damage index (*score or ID*) must be calculated for each individual and, in turn, for each treatment (averaging the data of the 10-15 individuals).

The manual recording carried out by the laboratory starts with photographic records taken through cameras attached to the microscope. It includes notebook entries of the number of cells in each class and then the transfer of the data to a spreadsheet for the computation of the *DNA* damage index (*score or ID)*. Nowadays, when talking about digital image processing, a large number of techniques and developments are constantly being improved, including the ability to segment and classify an image by treating it as an object.

Semantic segmentation at the instance level or instance segmentation, for example, is the task of detecting and jointly segmenting individual instances of objects in an image [2].

Neuro-fuzzy systems [3], [4] allow working on digital images through an operation that facilitates the processes of segmentation and pattern identification, both for recognition and interpretation tasks, as well as for object classification. [5]as well as object classification. [6].

The research begins with the possibility of obtaining digital images in the General Cytogenetics and Environmental Monitoring Laboratory through the use of an epifluorescence microscope and an attached camera.

The aim of the digital processing of these images, as proposed in this research, is to extract useful information that can be parameterised according to the Comet Test technique.

1.2 Objectives of the work

The main objective of this thesis is to develop a procedure that allows the capture, management and analysis of images of cellular samples, their self-classification into groups of belonging and analysis of data obtained in certain periods (defined by the user) for subsequent study in the Cytogenetics Laboratory of the Institute of Subtropical Biology of the Faculty of Exact, Chemical and Natural Sciences (IBS-UNaM-CONICET).

In order to achieve the above-mentioned objective, it is proposed to:

- To achieve self-classification of the images obtained, to determine the 5 groups (considering the anomalous ones within class 4), using neural networks, neuro-fuzzy algorithms and finally genetic functions or algorithms for their adjustment in order to obtain statistical and accurate data.
- To generate a prototypical procedure (development of a bioinformatics tool with Matlab®) that allows to clearly define the way of working by applying this type of image pattern recognition on the cytogenetic images obtained by applying the comet assay through fluorescence microscopy.

- Validate the prototype through the case study at the General Cytogenetics and Environmental Monitoring Laboratory of the Institute of Subtropical Biology.

1.3 Approach and method

For the improvement of the results of the observation of the images obtained through the Comet Assay in fluorescence microscopy - capture, classification, and management of the results in the development of the prototype - digital techniques are proposed that combine mathematical and computational algorithms in one line of study, which include fuzzy logic, fuzzy logic, fuzzy logic, fuzzy logic, fuzzy logic, fuzzy logic and fuzzy logic. [7], [8]neural networks [9] [10]convolutional [11], transfer learning, following the path of artificial intelligence (AI) [12], and *deep learning* [2][9].

In this implementation, the method that performs image pattern recognition efficiently will be selected.

The same technique can be employed to other case studies, enriched with knowledge management. [13]. Once the knowledge is acquired, it is possible to apply it to solve other problems in the field.

So far, different sources of information have been studied and analysed in order to define those image classification techniques with the least human intervention in image processing.

The expected outcome of this final master's degree work is the design and development of a prototype based on the image manipulation technique best suited to the specifications of the General Cytogenetics and Environmental Monitoring Laboratory of the UNaM-IBS-CONICET.

To realise this prototype, many techniques were evaluated, some were rejected because the development would serve a very particular case, others because they were applicable to industrial cases, others because they were too costly to implement or too cumbersome to develop. Finally, the use of neural networks and fuzzy logic systems were the simplest choice to implement and to carry out through a very functional prototype developed in Matlab®.

This Artificial Intelligence technology allows us to:

- *Adaptive learning*, i.e. learning based on initial experience. Training examples are very important.
- *Self-organisation:* a neural network can create its own organisation by learning.
- *Fault tolerance:* if any part of the network is damaged (even if the damage is extensive) some learned functions can still be recovered and only the system is degraded, not everything is lost.
- *Real-time operation and easy insertion into modular systems:* as specialised chips and hardware are available for neural networks to enhance their capability in the task.

Fuzzy Systems can be defined as precise algorithms, which describe imprecise relationships between objects. Through linguistic descriptions, relationships between input data and expected output data are defined, eliminating the excess precision inherent in mathematical modelling.

This feature helps us to deal with concepts of vagueness, imprecision and uncertainty. The second feature that improves is low-cost learning to adapt to individual preferences and environments.

Some characteristics that we can mention about fuzzy systems are:

- They formally represent the ambiguity and subjectivity of human thought.
- They model real complex problems in relevant applications:
  - Pattern recognition.
  - Prediction.
  - Control.
  - Assistance in decision-making.

1.4 Brief description of the other chapters of the report

The final paper is organised as follows:

In the first part (chapters 1 to 3) the concepts necessary for the development of the final master's thesis are incorporated. The theoretical framework is developed by evaluating different methods that can solve the problem, knowing them in depth and highlighting their differentiating aspects and conceptual justification. A brief mention of the mathematical foundations necessary for the development of the theory and a detailed description of the relevant aspects of this tool are also presented.

The approach and selection of methods allows for the development of:

Resolution through function-enhanced *fuzzy* hybrid algorithms developed in MATLAB® and GNU Octave.

From chapter 4 onwards, the development of the tool, i.e. the proposed solution, is described.

As future lines to follow, the final solution is proposed to be produced through a Smartphone application, improved with specific filters that allow the fluorescence to be treated and also to extend its use to human cells.

The final master's thesis is organised as follows:

State of the Art: Current knowledge is analysed with respect to the subject to be addressed in both the problem and the solution. Concepts are incorporated with which the final work is developed and which represent advantages and disadvantages with respect to their use in the final solution.

Artificial Intelligence in Image Pattern Recognition: Theory that frames and supports the chosen solution. Development of chosen models and algorithms. Artificial Neural Networks, their structures, learning, training and other important aspects such as convergence of processes and description of architectures and neuro-fuzzy system.

Models chosen: justification of the choice of methods and algorithms for solution development.

Development of the tool: Description of the development, models, mathematical algorithms, images of the different stages.

Results and Discussion: The realisation of the prototype results in a knowledge of new technologies and the ability to reproduce very accurately the selection and classification of images that could only be performed by the expertise of a geneticist. After a first training with a specific data *set* (*dataset*) and classified by hand, followed by a training with a *test set* consisting of several species. The programming of the algorithm allows us to automate the classification, in addition to having a historical record and the creation of a specific dataset.

Conclusions: With the proposal of this final master's thesis we sought to automate the classification of animal cells (fish and bivalves) in fluorescence tests, improving the time invested by the specialist in the Cytogenetics and Environmental Monitoring Laboratory and achieving a very effective optimisation in the classification of different types of cells. Through the study of different methodologies, their applicability was evaluated, first with empirical characteristic tests and then validating them with the case study. With the application of neuro-fuzzy algorithms, a very effective optimisation in the classification of different cell types was achieved. This was one of the problems that generated a very important limitation given that many models only allowed the classification of *DNA* from a single species. It should be noted that in this study, the model was prepared to classify *DNA* from different species of fish and bivalves with 93% accuracy.

Future lines: Description of the lines for future analysis based on improvements to the case study and the possibility of expanding it to other studies in human cells and to image management in general.

2

State of the Art

State of the Art

2.1 State of the art of the comet trial

It was not until the 1960s that pollution became internationally relevant due to the problems caused to man and his environment. Interest in these issues intensified even more in recent decades due to the occurrence of accidents involving chemical products that had worldwide repercussions. The first actions to understand the causes and undesirable effects of different toxic agents have arisen.[15].

The emergence of specialised disciplines such as Ecotoxicology and toxicological genetics that developed around scientific, technological and practical objectives; and the political interest of the United Nations manifested since 1992 at the World Conference on Development and Environment, allowed the adoption of a Sustainable Development plan for the 21st century, which included social, economic and ecological aspects of all public domains both at local and regional, national and international levels.[16] .

These different scenarios led to the emergence of Environmental Risk Assessment (ERA) studies, which became prevalent as experts and the general public realised that certain chemicals, non-toxic to human health, can have adverse effects on natural resources. These studies involve the identification and characterisation of risk, as well as the likelihood of occurrence of adverse effects on all components of the ecosystem.[16].

Environmental monitoring is one of the main steps in environmental risk assessment, which consists of the repetitive observation of one or more chemical or biological elements, based on defined objectives within an organised scheme in time and space, using comparable and standardised methods. To assess the risk posed by environmental pollutants on organisms and to classify the quality of different environments, monitoring can focus on physicochemical components (Physicochemical Monitoring) or on biological components at all levels (Biological Monitoring or Biomonitoring).[16].

Biomonitoring is performed through biomarkers, which detect and reflect changes in biological responses (variables) induced by the presence of environmental pollutants, manifested through variations in cellular and biochemical components, as well as variations in structures or functions determinable in an organism (biomarker) or a sample thereof. They are early warning signals reflecting adverse biological responses to the action of a pollutant and are characterised by their sensitivity, biological relevance and feasibility.[16].

Among the techniques available to assess DNA damage, the Comet Assay or *Single Cell Gel Electrophoresis* has become one of the methods of choice. This assay was initially described as a microgel electrophoresis technique to detect *DNA* damage at the single cell level. [17][18].

The Comet Assay technique using fluorescence microscopy as a medium and tool plays an important role in research and is a widely used technique. This assay is based on the structure and organisation of *DNA* within the nucleus, where the cells under study are exposed to a chemical solution on a slide, the cell membranes, cytoplasm and nucleoplasm are removed. "The resulting structure is called a nucleoid and is the *DNA* stripped of histone proteins, the size of the original nucleus of the cell". This *DNA* is denatured in an alkaline solution for a sufficient period of time to expose the presence of breaks in its strands as a result of exposure to contaminants, which causes a relaxation of the supercoiling in its structure. The greater the number of breaks in the *DNA* strands, the greater the degree of relaxation of the strands. When these nucleoids are subjected to electrophoresis, the negatively charged *DNA* will migrate towards the anode. After neutralising and fixing the preparations, staining with specific *DNA-binding* fluorescent dyes will reveal images resembling "comets", a characteristic that gives the technique its name. Therefore, the ability of *DNA* to migrate and originate comets will depend on both the size and the number of breaks that occur in its strands. The greater the damage, the longer and more intensely coloured the comets' tails will be in relation to the comets' heads. [16][18].

After the assay, the images resulting from the microscopy analysis are recorded. In the laboratory, these tasks are so far performed manually with cameras that capture the images in total darkness and the trained eye of the geneticist classifies the images.

One of the main research objectives of the laboratory is to assess the impact of freshwater environments with different levels of contamination on the *DNA* of different bioindicator organisms. [19].

With this cytogenetic-molecular technique it is also possible to analyse different cell types in the same individual, providing more detailed information on the environmental impact as it makes it possible to assess DNA damage in various tissues and organs, which react differently to different environmental pollutants.[20].

The problem of river pollution has led specialists to explore innovative tools for the assessment of effluents in surface waters. One of the alternatives that is gaining relevance is the use of macroinvertebrates (bivalve molluscs) and lower vertebrates (fish, amphibians) as bioindicators. This is due to their distribution and sedentarism, sensitivity to environmental disturbances, long life cycles in water (in the case of macroinvertebrates), and because of their ecological characteristics and their position in the food chain. For all these reasons, they are good bioaccumulators of environmental substances (mainly organic compounds). [16].

Bioconcentration and bioaccumulation of substances occur when an organism ingests chemical contaminants from its environment and through food, respectively. These pollutants accumulate in tissues and through the trophic chain, through a process of biomagnification, increase in concentration in organisms higher up the food chain, and may ultimately impact on the humans that feed on them. [16].

This environmental study through biomonitoring is a widely used alternative as it is simple, low-cost and with highly reliable results.

2.2 State of the art imaging in environmental monitoring

The incorporation of neural networks in a hierarchical and partitioned manner into the image processing of environmental study images has been underway since 2008 [21][22].

In 2009, a differential evolution algorithm for macroinvertebrate recognition is developed. This consists of a self-adaptive scheme with two local search algorithms, which detect and assign a value to an offspring. These processes aid in global search that provide improved solutions as a precursor to what we can use today. [23]. They give more flexibility to the problem by having two search algorithms and not just one.

These algorithms use the support vector machine technique which is a representation of data as points scattered in space in a way that facilitates a binary classification, then in 2009 a two and three dimensional pattern recognition system is proposed[24].

The implementation of convolutional neural networks (*CNNs*) is fundamentally manifested since 1998 with a seminal paper [25] presenting the most relevant ideas about image recognition using convolutional trained multilayer neural networks and backpropagation applied to handwriting pattern recognition, which exemplify a successful gradient-based learning technique. Given a suitable network architecture, gradient-based learning algorithms can be used to synthesise a complex decision surface that can classify high-dimensional patterns, such as handwritten characters, with minimal pre-processing. This paper reviews several methods applied to handwritten character recognition and compares them on a standard handwritten digit, whose success is based on the evolution of computational power.[25].

In 2012, *Alex net*'s development of a neural network, achieved a 15% error rate in image identification for the Imagenet large-scale visual recognition competition (*ILSVRC*). With this procedure, it achieved a remarkable advance over its rival, which scored 25%, and clearly determined its superiority.[26]. The development of precision deep learning techniques in 2015 achieved a 4.8% performance, exceeding human accuracy in the same test.[27].

Manual analysis, can be tedious and exposed to the bias of the professional who analyses it, which makes one consider the use of other methods to obtain indicators after the visual analysis of the samples, such as artificial intelligence or data mining. [26][27][28].

The development of this automation prototype to classify cytogenetic images according to their DNA damage, aims to improve analysis times and the possibility of creating a history of the results, also taking into account the standardisation of the photos of the samples so that when comparing them all are classified with an equalised histogram. Also to evaluate how this procedure can be optimised by using some Genetic algorithms [29]Neuro Fuzzy, Neuro Fuzzy[30]or Neuro Convolutional Networks (CNN). [24].

At the moment the methods available to recognise the images presented by the microscope, so that these images can be captured, processed and analysed through digital mechanisms, are diverse[31].

In the literature reviewed, developments in digital image processing in different fields, such as engineering, biology, medicine, etc., were found. However, there are not many references on genetics or cytogenetics with learning algorithms.

Digital image processing is computer-based imaging and is the images obtained within the visible range of the electromagnetic spectrum, acoustic, electronic, and synthetic images. [32].

Advancement in this area does not happen on its own but always goes hand in hand with other disciplines with which it is associated such as mathematics and computing and is reflected in biology, mechanics, medicine, geology mining, astronomy etc. [33][34].

Imaging treatments are multivariate. For example, in histopathology, new technology is incorporated into image analysis, not only through computers but also through smartphones, which offers the advantage of collecting and storing photographic records, and their immediate subsequent classification through the use of the application developed for this purpose. [35] which offers as an advantage the collection and storage of photographic records, and their immediate subsequent classification through the use of the application developed for this purpose. There is software developed such as "Komet 7®" that captures and analyses comets, calculates internationally accepted measurements (it has certification) and generates statistics, or Capslab, which is a comet testing software project that fulfils the functions proposed in this research, some of which are freely distributed and others are proprietary developments.

At the basis of all developments and procedures, mathematical algorithms are used to support neural networks, neuro-fuzzy systems and Artificial Intelligence [33][36].

Fuzzy reasoning driven by NN Hideyuki Takagi and Isao Hayashi Matsushita Electric Industrial Co. is chosen because it can solve two problems of conventional fuzzy reasoning by combining an artificial neural network and fuzzy reasoning, [4] because it can solve two problems of conventional fuzzy reasoning by combining an artificial neural network and fuzzy reasoning, which also allows fixing the inference rules and adjustment according to the time-varying reasoning environment. This proposed method can be applied to network modelling and artificial intelligence, and is considered to incorporate knowledge into the neural network structure. [4].

Fuzzy reasoning mimics human logic reasoning in its flexibility. Its applications are seen in the fields of control, artificial intelligence and operations research. It is not a set of rules that achieve smooth control with slight variations, but it also provides a certain flexibility as in human logic itself.

Fuzzy control is a control rule of humanreasoning expressed in human words, It manages to represent in a fuzzy or fuzzy rule concepts such as "speed should be gradually reduced", which also decreases the number of rules and to execute it, the relationship between the input data obtained through sensors and the different fuzzy sets must be determined. This mapping relationship is a membership function. The main strength of the method is the achievement of gathering the logical rules and contextualising them in fuzzy sets through membership functions (the function is in charge of classifying the elements of confusion intertwined in the logic, or in other words, it classifies through clear rules formally representing the ambiguity of human thought through the modelling of real complex problems). [37].

The second feature that improves is low-cost learning to suit individual preferences and environments.

Neural networks can handle two problems in fuzzy reasoning. The difference between these two technologies has to do with whether the logic is explicit or implicit. For fuzzy reasoning, stable reasoning can always be achieved despite data deviations, because the logic of the backbone manifests itself as a rule of the form IF-THEN and the rule cannot be expressed if the logic is not identified. As the neural network self-organises the mapping relationship during learning, it can be applied to unknown, non-linear relationships because it is itself non-linear. At the same time it requires a large amount of data. If in learning, the data is wrong, it can detract from the learning. [4].

Then fuzzy reasoning is used for well-identified logical cases such as control and neural networks for unidentified recognition rules such as pattern recognition [6].

The methods chosen in this final master's thesis are neural networks and neuro-fuzzy systems, due to the fact that when classifying the images of the cells obtained through the Comet Assay, the fuzzy head and tail will not always fit exactly into one or the other class, no matter how much detail you have when defining it and examining it. The fact that it is a biological material means that it has its own characteristics, even if they vary from individual to individual, are characteristics that invite the use of a neuro-fuzzy system. The adjustment of values with genetic algorithms, or through functions, allows to improve the global performance and to arrive at more accurate results.[4].

With this choice, the algorithm is able to detect nuclei and classify them beyond the species under study (in this case two species of fish and bivalves), which allows it to handle a certain flexibility that is very convenient in this type of cytogenetic analysis, so that the results obtained can be applied to other cases.

3

Artificial Intelligence in Image Pattern Recognition

3.1 Problems recognising an image

The problems to be faced when designing an application using Computer Vision technology, algorithms or Artificial Intelligence are complex. Since in the development of algorithms, images constitute a matrix of numbers, applications will have to translate those numbers into objects.

It must also be taken into account that the objects of study will present a very different set of appearances in the image, since it will depend, for example, on the point of view that will make them appear rotated, moved to one area of the image or to another, or more or less large. And despite these changes, the algorithm has to know that it is the same type of object.

In addition, it may be the case that the image sought does not have a shape with symmetrical, continuous or clearly defined contours, for example a cell, so that it presents changes due to the position or simply because it is not exactly the same as one another. Another very important factor is the lighting, which may not be constant, and which will not only make the images look lighter or darker, but may also generate shadows, modify the contrast between different areas, and so on.

In an application it may be that the object of study is together with other objects in the analysed image. The presence of other objects may cause occlusions, so that the image of interest will not be seen as a whole but only parts of it.

The search is also complicated if there are differences in the possible fields of observation according to the species under study, so it is essential to define the search criteria specifically and what characteristics you want to look for in the image. In addition, there is usually a very demanding time constraint.

And in that time, the possible results in each image are examined, so that if a single algorithm works at 99.9% accuracy, you will have several discarded or wrong results per image.

These errors will be false positives, i.e. when it is claimed that the objects being searched for are present in the image and they are not. Otherwise, false negatives, which is when they are not detected even though they are present.

There are currently many methods that support these actions, both in *Machine learning* and *Deep learning*[38][39].

The human neuron gave rise to the creation of artificial intelligence processes through the discovery of mechanisms governing the morphology and connective processes of nerve cells. [40]

Neural networks propose a way to emulate certain human characteristics, such as the ability to memorise and associate facts. If you look closely at those problems that cannot be expressed through an algorithm, you will see that they all have one characteristic in common: experience. Man is able to solve these situations by drawing on accumulated experience. Thus, it seems clear that one way of approaching the problem is to build systems that are capable of reproducing this human characteristic. [41].

In short, neural networks are nothing more than an artificial and simplified model of the human brain, which is the most perfect example we have for a system that is capable of acquiring knowledge through experience. A neural network is "a new system for information processing, whose basic processing unit is inspired by the fundamental cell of the human nervous system: the neuron". [41].

The process that occurs is that the neuron is stimulated or excited through its inputs and when a threshold is reached, the neuron is activated by passing a signal to the axon.

This is because an electrochemical process is further developed. [42].

Intelligence occurs in this context of interrelationships between millions of neurons and learning as the experience of new pathways or new connections created through new stimuli. Neural networks then consist of processing units that exchange data or information. Through them, patterns can be recognised, including images, signals, scripts and timelines (trends and projections) with the ability to learn and improve processes. [25].

Definitions vary according to the context in which they are defined, but they always arise from inspiration in biological models and allow results to be obtained through the application of mathematical or statistical processes, in which data are organised by levels and outputs are the result of the interactions of simple interconnected elements and processes that also attempt to relate to the real world [43].

Just as the brain is able to learn from experience, similar features in Artificial Intelligence allow it to abstract essential points of commonality from inputs that represent irrelevant information. Neural networks can recognise data or images they have never seen before by generalising the input information and self-organising, recognising certain features by assembling patterns. [44]

While they have similar characteristics to the brain, (they are able to learn, to generalise new cases based on previous cases, they can abstract essential features from input data) they also have very different characteristics; brain circuits do not implement recursive computation and are therefore not algorithmic. Although an algorithm, by definition, can define recursive functions.

The basic computational unit of a neural network, the neuron, receives an electrical input signal and when it reaches a certain threshold, it is transformed to generate a new electrical output signal as shown (Fig. 1). This transformation is performed in the model through activation functions, the most common of which are step, sigmoid, RELU, Gaussian functions.

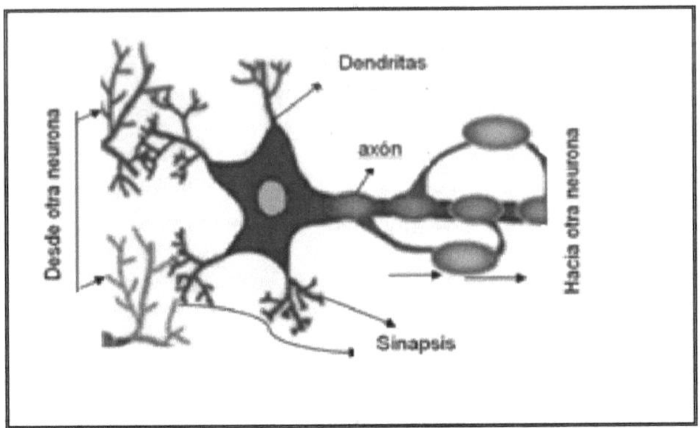

Figure 1Graphical representation of the connective processes of the biological neuron showing the synapses

The neuron receives information from some nodes, or from an external source, and generates an output. Each input has an associated weight (w), which is assigned according to its importance relative to other inputs (Fig. 2). The node applies an activation function, e.g. sigmoid, Hyperbolic Tangent or RELU to the weighted sum of its inputs. If the combined signal is not large enough, the effect of the sigmoid threshold function is to suppress the output signal and trigger otherwise.

In a biological neural network, dendrites collect electrical signals and combine to form a stronger signal. If the signal is strong and exceeds the threshold, the neuron fires a signal down the axon to the terminals to pass on to the dendrites of the next neuron. It is important to note that each neuron receives information from many previous neurons and also provides signals to many more. One way to replicate this phenomenon in nature using an artificial model is to have layers of neurons, each connected to each other in the anterior and posterior layer. The diagram below (Fig. 2) illustrates this idea:

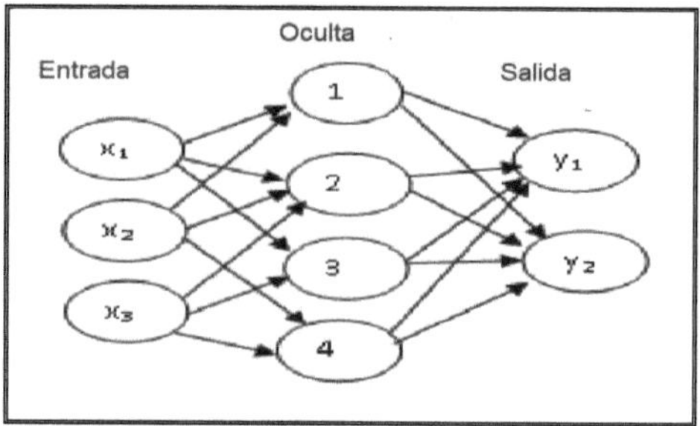

Figure 2Different layers feeding a neuron and how the signals accumulate.

In a Deep Learning architecture, a single neuron produces transformations in the data in the following way:

$X \rightarrow$ $y = f \rightarrow (\omega.x + b)$ where the data in brackets make the first transformation and then through the activation functions that are not linear the outputs are provoked.

In the linear function of the form *Z=WX+b with W being the weight associated with the inputs and Z the output or action* (i.e. the neurons do not react only on contact with the stimulus), it is apparent that the neurons do not react readily but suppress the input until the intensity of the stimulus has grown so great that an output is triggered.

This is where the trigger function appears. It is a function that takes the input signal and generates the output signal but takes into account some kind of threshold.

Some activation functions are as follows:

Table 1 Activation functions:

Función	Formula	Rango
Identidad	$y = x$	$[-\infty, \infty]$
Escalón	$y = \begin{cases} +1 & \text{si } x \geq 0 \\ 0 & \text{si } x < 0 \end{cases}$	$[0,1]$
	$y = \begin{cases} +1 & \text{si } x \geq 0 \\ -1 & \text{si } x < 0 \end{cases}$	$[-1,1]$
Lineal a tramos	$y = \begin{cases} x & \text{si } -1 \leq x \leq 1 \\ +1 & \text{si } x > 1 \\ -1 & \text{si } x < -1 \end{cases}$	$[-1,1]$
Sigmoidea	$y = \dfrac{1}{1+e^{-x}}$	$[0,1]$
	$y = \tanh(x)$	$[-1,1]$
Sinusoidal	$y = Sen(\omega.x + \varphi)$	$[-1,1]$

The **Step** function, where the output is zero for low input values. But once it reaches the threshold, the output increases. The step function can be improved in many ways, the threshold is given by the sum of the weights of the inputs.

The **S-shaped function** shown in (Fig. 3) is called **sigmoid** or **logistic** function. Its form is:

$$f(z) = \frac{1}{1+e^{-z}} \qquad\qquad (1)$$

This function basically classifies into two classes, 0 and 1.

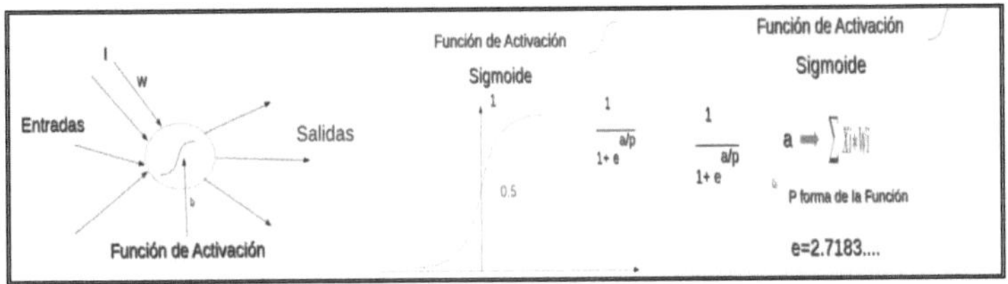

Figure 3 Sigmoid or logistic activation function of a neuron where a is the sum of the inputs times their weights and p is the shape of the function.

Another very important activation function that is widely used is **ReLU** fig. 4 or *rectified linear unit* activation function, whose equation is:

$$R(z) = Max(0, z) \qquad\qquad (2)$$

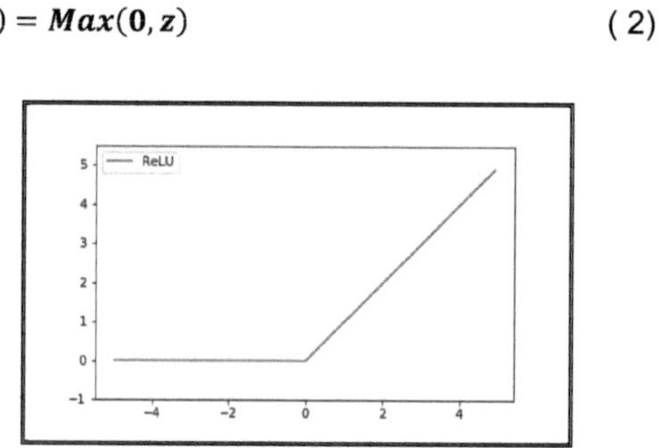

Figure 4 Rectified linear unit function.

There are different types of activation functions. In the prototype developed, the sigmoid function has been used to perform image classification.

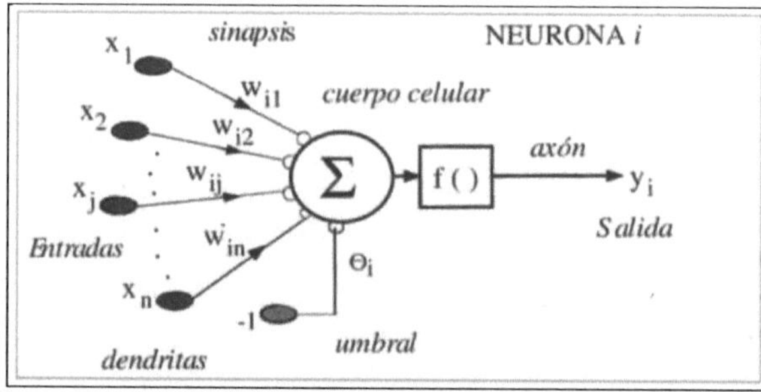

Figure 5 Neuron and action-activating functions.

In a first instance one of the chosen lines of research was the topology of self-organised polynomial neural networks (*SOPNN*) based on the genetically optimised multilayer perceptron (*MLP*), an interesting option to use. In the design of "conventional" *SOPNNNs, the* extended group method of data handling (*GMDH*) technique is used to consider the fixed nodes that make up the input of each layer. However, this learning does not always result in the optimal architecture, so the design procedure applied in the construction of each layer, taking into account the specific characteristics and optimisation of parameters, also proposes a performance index with a weighting factor that allows a balance between approximations and generalisations or predictions. It is a model with accuracy and predictive capability. This supervised ontogenetic neural network topology called Self-Optimising Neural Networks (SONN) (Fig. 6) has characteristic multilayer neural networks, with connections that are achieved through an adaptation process based on the training data provided. The process is able to extract the most general and discriminative features from the data and create only the main connections (neurons), automatically reducing the training input data vectors, thus avoiding dimensionality problems. [33].

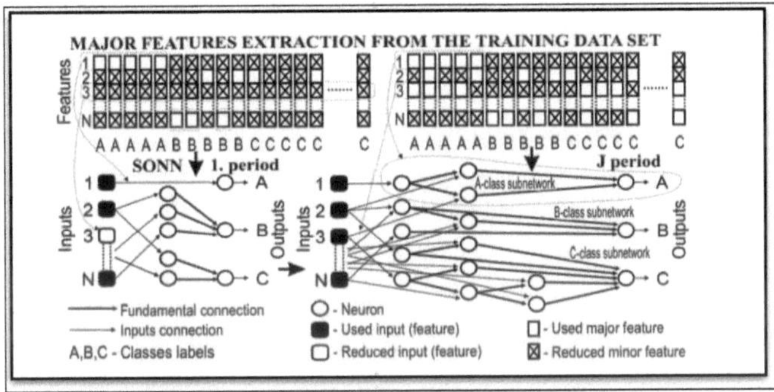

Figure 6SONN development based on feature discrimination. Source: [37] "Neural network designed on approximate reasoning architecture and their Applications Hideyuki Takagi and Isao Hayashi Matsushita Electric Industrial Co. SONN automatically and simultaneously adapts the topology of the NN and all its weights in the deterministic process.

Fuzzy reasoning(Fig. 6) can solve the problems of conventional fuzzy reasoning through artificial neural network and fuzzy reasoning, to achieve the design of membership function and The flexibility of adapting to the reasoning environment.[4].

The fuzzy reasoning approach solves them using a learning function and a neural network, being able to determine rules of inferences and adjustment according to the time-varying reasoning environment due to the use of neural network in fuzzy reasoning. This proposed method can be applied to neural network modelling and artificial intelligence, incorporating knowledge into the neural network structure.[4].

Fuzzy reasoning mimics the reasoning of human logic, and this flexibility - of fundamental importance when applied to living material - was defining in the choice of method for the solution algorithm.

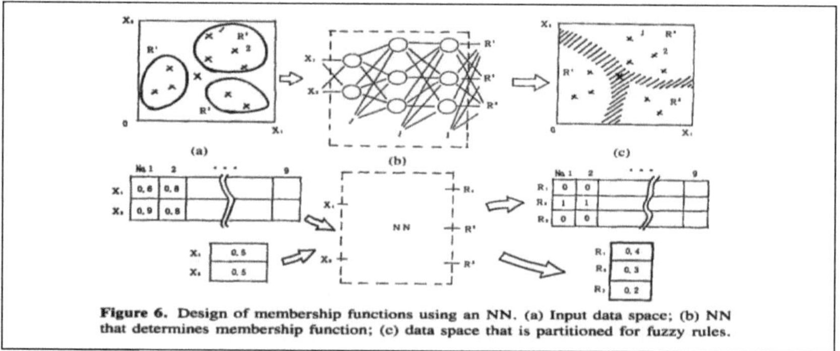

Figure 6. Design of membership functions using an NN. (a) Input data space; (b) NN that determines membership function; (c) data space that is partitioned for fuzzy rules.

Figure 7 Fuzzy reasoning [4] H Takagi and I. Hayashi "Nn Driven fuzzy reasoning".

Thus, as shown in Fig. 7, the solution to the problem posed in the Cytogenetics Laboratory (UNaM-IBS- CONICET) is found within neural networks and fuzzy sets. This hybrid, neuro-fuzzy method was selected for its flexibility, simplicity of execution and, above all, for the simplicity of the prototype after applying some functions and algorithms.

3.2 Neural Networks en

This is a neural network with three layers, each with several neurons or artificial nodes, where each node is connected to any other node in the previous and following layers. In this way we take the idea of the human brain and apply it to build a neural architecture for computers. Learning is done by adjusting the strength of the connections between nodes through mathematical algorithms. Within a node, we adjust the sum of the inputs, or the shape of the sigmoid threshold function, but this is more complicated than simply adjusting the strength of the connections between nodes. Fig. 7 shows the connected nodes, but this time the weight associated with each connection is shown. A low weight will disregard a signal and a high weight will amplify it.

The idea of calculating signals in a neural network from the inputs through the different layers to become the output is called neural network feedforward. It consists of a Boolean function represented by the formula :

$$F(x,y,z)=xy+ z^{\leftarrow} \tag{3}$$

The values of this function given below are used to perform the neural network operations through equation 3:

Table 2 Function values for performing neural network operations .

X	Y	Z	xy	zZ	$f(x,y,z)=xy+z^{\leftarrow}$
1	1	1	1	0	1
1	1	0	1	1	1
1	0	1	0	0	0
1	0	0	0	1	1
0	1	1	0	0	0
0	1	0	0	1	1
0	0	1	0	0	0
0	0	0	0	1	1

The fourth row depicted in table 2 ((1, 0, 1) ≥ 0) is used to demonstrate the pre-feed, where (1, 0, 1) ≥ 0 shows the direct feed.

The first layer is called the input layer and the last layer is called the output layer. The layers in between are called hidden layers. The input and hidden layers contain three nodes and the output layer contains only one node. If weights are assigned to the synapses between the input and the hidden layer, the weights are taken randomly between (0) and (1) as this is the first time the network is fed Fig. 8.

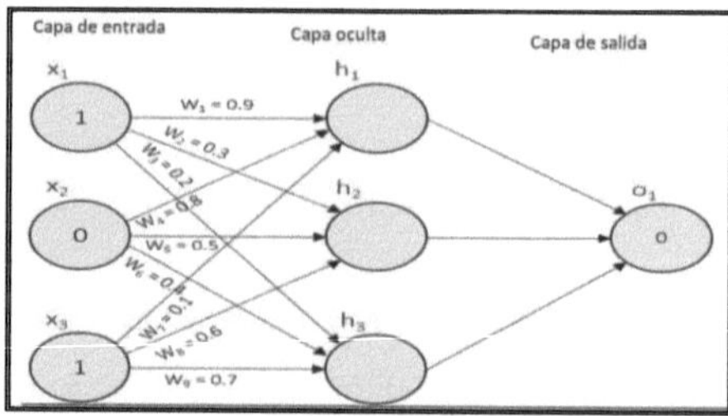

Figure 8 Neural Network, pre-feed.

As a single neuron or node works, we take all the inputs and multiply them with the associated weights, finally summing them. Then, the node applies an activation function, such as sigmoid, to the weighted sum of its inputs to introduce non-linearity.

This process is repeated for several layers and for each node in these layers.

All nodes in the input layer are connected to the hidden layer and those input nodes have raw values of the associated weights as seen in equation 4.

$$Z = \sum w_{y0} \, x_{y0} \tag{4}$$

$$d(Z) = \frac{1}{1 + e^{\square\square - z}}$$

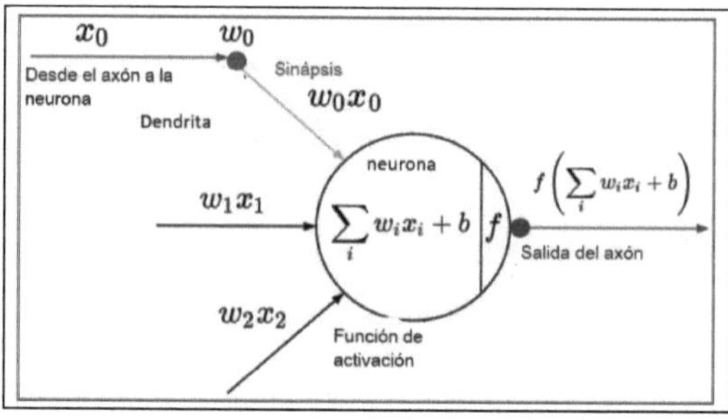

Figure 9Modification of a single neuron from input values, weights and output values after applying the function.

The small sums are in the circle because they are not the final value. That output node value is calculated using the activation function. Applied to the three weighted hidden layer sums we get the neural network hidden layer value Fig.9 and then applied to the hidden layer results with the second set of weights (randomly determined) we get the output sum,:

$$f(z) = \frac{1}{1+e^{-z}} \tag{5}$$

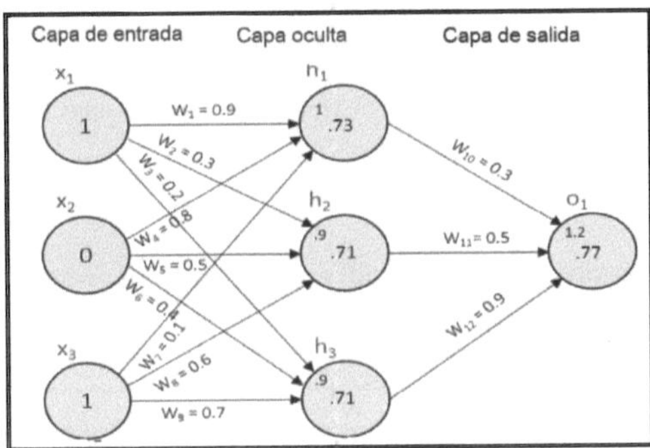

Figure 10Neural Network: pre-training calculations.

When applying the sigmoid activation function to obtain the final output result and using a random set of initial weights, the value of the output neuron is out of range; in this case e.g. +0.77 (since the target is 0).

$$\sigma(1.213) = 0.7708293339958$$

Then, far from the target value the network has to be trained to calibrate the weights or values obtained Fig. 10, to calculate the *feedforward* process also called *feedforward* neural network, matrix computation is used. The process to calibrate the weights is backpropagation Fig.11.

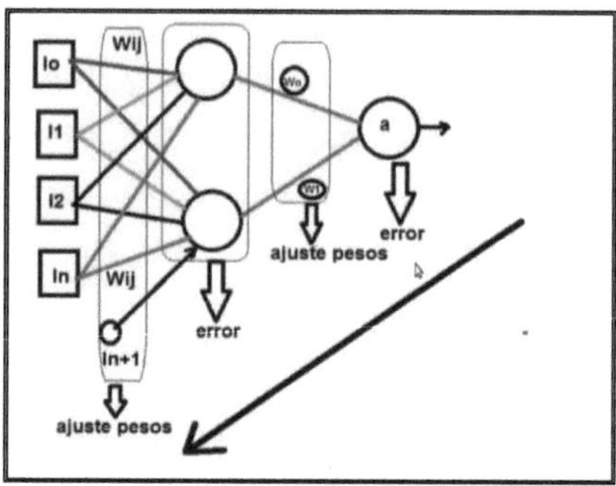

Figure 11Illustrative image of Neural Network with Three layers and weights represented with back propagation.

Matrices in the neural network

A matrix has the following form of a table with numbers, where the values of the matrix are the neural network weights

W_{11}	W_{21}	W_{31}
W_{12}	W_{22}	W_{32}
W_{13}	W_{23}	W_{33}

The network inputs can be represented by another matrix. By multiplying both matrices, the inputs are obtained:

Input 1
Input 2
Input 3

With the weighted sum of the input and the hidden layer, then, the output of the hidden layer can be calculated: where W is the weight matrix and x is the input matrix.

This technique is called **vectorisation**. Artificial intelligence allows for adaptive learning, self-organisation, fault tolerance, real-time operation and easy insertion into modular systems.

In *Adaptive Learning,* networks learn to differentiate patterns through examples and training and are self-adaptive systems. They are adaptive because they can adjust to new learning by developing new hierarchies. They are dynamic because they can be constantly changing and this is fundamental as they do not always need an algorithm that considers all circumstances, but can create their weight distribution based on learning. Some networks learn all their lives, even after their training period is completed, you just need to provide training with patterns.

Thus, we speak of self-organisation when networks use adaptive learning to self-organise the information they receive during learning in order to achieve a specific goal.

Backpropagation, or *backpropagation*, generates its characteristic organisation that allows it to recognise certain patterns and at the same time allows it to generalise behaviours. This is useful when the input data is partially defined or incompletely defined. This name is given because the error is propagated from the output layer backwards (i.e. it corrects the errors until it reaches the input layer, adjusting the values of the input data). This allows the weights on the connections of the neurons in the hidden layers to change state during training. The change of the weights influences the global input, activation and consequently the output of the neuron.

To carry out the diagnosis of the case study, detection and segmentation of the cell nucleus or the cell as a whole is necessary. Regardless of the way the information is processed, it is difficult to find a sufficiently robust and accurate method.

Neural Network models are neurons connected to each other and working together, without a specific task for each one. With experience, the neurons create and reinforce certain connections in order to learn, and these connections become fixed in the fabric. While the first sense is biological, it is based on mathematics, statistics and computer algorithms. It is based on a simple idea: given some parameters, there is a way to combine them to achieve a certain result.

Neural networks allow you to find the combination of parameters that best fits a given problem. They are a model for finding that combination of parameters and applying it at the same time.

For this the neural network must be trained, an already trained network can be used to make classifications or predictions, i.e., to apply the combination [44].

Several kernel detection methods are used in the literature, which can be subdivided according to the main algorithm used. Methods using the morphological operation distance transform, maximum/minimum H-transform, Laplacian Guadiana filter [45]maximum stable extreme region detection, Hough transform, radial symmetry based voting, maximum stable extreme region detection, Hough transform [46]radial symmetry based voting; as well as supervised learning methods can also be found. [47], Support vector machine [22]Reinforcement learning [48] and deep neural networks [49]. Some of these methods (such as the Hough transform), we will see that they are used in the prototype developed in this research (in chapter 4 p. 55).

Segmentation, on the other hand, attempts to delimit objects across boundaries. Three strategies stand out for carrying out the separation of the nucleus from the cells:

First: separate the background from the plane.

Second: Identify the core indicators and then expand their boundaries.

Third: generate candidate regions and then select the best ones to be segmented. The most commonly used segmentation algorithms are limit intensity, divisive transformation, K-means as a clustering method, whose fuzzy version is Fuzzy-C means clustering, expectation maximisation, graph-based methods and Fuzzy-C means clustering [48] [49]. [48]Fuzzy-C means clustering, expectation maximisation, graph-based methods and supervised classification (pixel classification: super pixel classification). [49]. Many of the approaches presented in the literature are not included for testing due to the inflexibility of these methods in the face of the intrinsic variability of images of biological material in microscopy. The type of sample and mode of preparation, as well as light, can influence and make the segmentation of cells/nuclei that are partially overlapping or stuck together a scientific challenge to solve.

3.3 Fuzzy Logic

Fuzzy reasoning [4]is the proposed reasoning approach, solves these problems by using the learning function and the nonlinearity of a neural network. First, the problems involved in conventional fuzzy reasoning and the neural network used in this paper are identified. Then, the proposed algorithm is formulated and a concrete explanation is developed using real data.

Fuzzy reasoning is able to automatically determine the rules of inference and adjustment according to the time-varying reasoning environment Fig. 12 and 13.

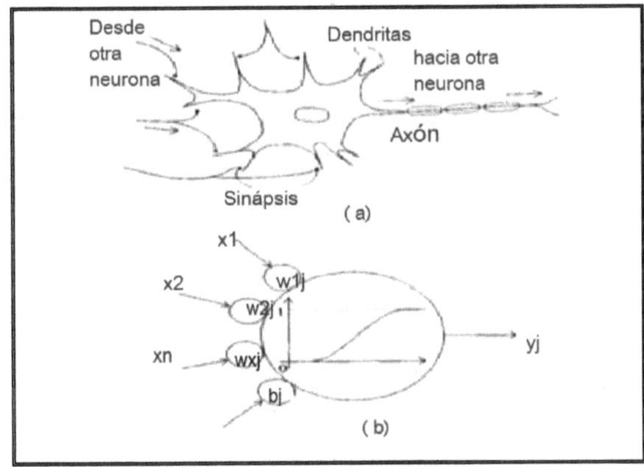

Figure 12NN driven Fuzzy reasoning, H.Takagiy I.Hayashi [4].

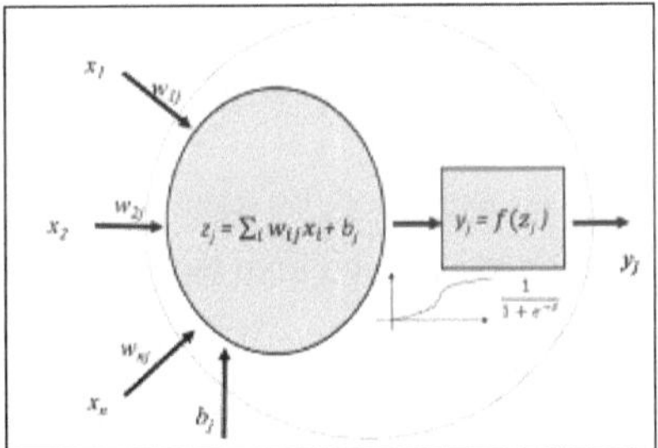

Figure 13Sigmoid function in neural networks, *fuzzy* reasoning (*fuzzy*). [4].

Fuzzy logic and fuzzy number algorithms allow to outline and differentiate areas in which they can determine class membership, without having all the characteristics that strictly correspond to this class. In the clustering method, the number of groups is equal to the number of rules that are inferred.

3.4 Neuro-fuzzy method

The fuzzy reasoning mentioned above can solve two problems of conventional fuzzy reasoning by combining an artificial neural network (NN) and Fuzzy reasoning. [4]:

- Design for membership function, heuristic approach only.
- Lack of flexibility in adapting to the reasoning environment.

The fuzzy reasoning approach solves them by means of a learning function of a neural network, furthermore it is able to determine inference rules and adjustment according to the time-varying reasoning environment, applied to modelling it is considered as incorporating knowledge into the neural network structure [4].

The main strength of the method is that it manages to bring together the logical rules and contextualise them in fuzzy sets through membership functions (the function is in charge of channelling through these more flexible rules, the data with functions intertwined in the logic).

The second feature that improves is low-cost learning to suit individual preferences and environments.

Fuzzy reasoning is then used for well-identified logical cases such as control and neural networks for unidentified recognition rules such as pattern recognition.

When designing the membership function, the inference function can be derived from fuzzy rules of the learning data using neural network learning, which also allows for function adaptation.

The outline of the method is explained by taking as an example the control performed by two inputs $x \sim$ and $x2$, derived from two sensors.

The algorithm consists of three main parts:

1. Rules of inference.

2. The identification of IF (*If*) (determination of a membership function).

3. The identification of *THEN* (the determination of the control event for each rule).

The first part is the determination of fuzzy inference rules and the combination of data belonging to each rule. These data are grouped by a clustering method and the number of groups is equal to the number of rules (See Fig. 7 page 36).

The second part is the determination of the arbitrary input for each rule, which defines the membership function for each rule and corresponds to the identification of the Si parts (rule condition) that combines the fuzzy parts. As shown in Fig. 7, in the SI-part the membership is formed using the explicit and flexible rules determined in the first part for each defined class. The neural network can form an arbitrary continuous function, which can even have a hidden layer.

The third part of the algorithm is the determination of the THEN (parts of the conclusion).

The neural network supervised by the learning data and the control value for each rule as in the second part. The detailed formulation of the neural network is explained in the following fuzzy modelling example [4] where the THEN part in the control system is responsible for inferring the exact control value. One such method is fuzzy modelling in the form: if "If x is A, THEN $y = u(x)$", where x is an input vector, A is the fuzzy set of partitioned rule spaces and $u(x)$ designates an inference function for the control operation.

- Step 1: being the input variables x_j , $j = 1.2$ ..... k. and the observed value, the output variable y_i . where the x_j , $j=1.2$ .....m, $m \leq k$ related to the observed value and are selected by the neural network. This is done by backpropagation or backward error elimination, using the sum of squared errors as a cost function to eliminate the input variables that have to do with noise and differentiate those that are actually inputs.

- Step 2: The input and output data (x_j , Y_i) are divided into training data (*TRN* of n_t) and verification data (*CHD* of n_c) for model estimation, where $n = n_t + n_c$.

- Step 3: The training partition is found by a clustering method. The best number is obtained by a clustering method and is decided in relation to the distance between the clusters in a cluster dendogram: (see Fig. 2). Each of the TRDs divided into r groups is expressed as R_s , $s=1,2...r$, and the TRDs of R^s are expressed by (x^s_i , y^s_i) where $i=1,2,...(n_t)^s$,and $(n_t)^s$ are numbers of TRDs in each R^s . The division of the n-dimensional space into r here means that the number of inference rules is r.

- Step 4: Is the identification of the constitution of each SI (*IF*) part in NN_{mem} (NN that generates the membership functions). If x_i are the values for the input layer, $w^s{}_i$ is assigned as supervised data for the output layer.

$$w_i s = \begin{cases} 1, \dots \dots x_i \notin \mathbf{R}_S \\ 0, \dots \dots x_i \in \mathbf{R}_S \end{cases}$$

where i=1,2, ... (n_t); s=1,.......r .

The learning of NN_{mem} is carried out so that these $w^s{}_i$ can be inferred from the input layer x, so that NN_{mem} becomes able to infer the degree of attribution $w^s{}_i$ of each training data item x_i to R^S . If the membership function of the IF part is the inferred value $w^s{}_i$ which is the result of the learned NN_{mem} , that is,

$$\mu_A{}^s\ (X_i\ ) \equiv w^s{}_i\ ,\ i=1,\dots..n.\ (6)$$

- Step 5: This is the identification of each THEN. The structure of each inference rule is expressed by the input/output relationship. The input TRD $x^s{}_{i1}$, ... $x^s{}_{im}$ and the output value $y^s{}_t$, i=1,2,....$(n_t\ )^s$ are mapped to the input and output NN_s . This NN_s is the NN of the THEN part in R^s . The training of NN_s is carried out in such a way that the control value can be inferred. The input values CHD x_{i1} , ... x_{im} i=1,2,....... n_c , are substituted into the NN to obtain the sum $\Theta^s{}_m$ of the squared errors.

$$\Theta_m^s = \sum_{i=1}^{nc}\{y_i - u_s(x_i).\mu_{A^s}\ (x_i)\}^2 \tag{7}$$

This estimated value $u_s\ (x_i\ )$ is obtained as the output NN_s. Another way of calculating Θ^s is with the weight; that means

$$\Theta_m^s = \sum_{i=1}^{nc} \mu_A^x(x_i)\{y_i - u_s(x_i).\mu_A^s(x_i)\}^2 \tag{8}$$

Using it to decide the best number of learning iterations of the neural network to prevent overtraining.

$$I^s = \frac{n_c}{n_t^s + n_c} \sum_{i=1}^{n_t^s} \{y_i - us(x_i)\}^2 + \frac{n_t^s}{n_t^s + n_c} \sum_{j=1}^{n_c} \{y_j - u_s(x_j) \cdot \mu_A^s(x_j)\}^2 \qquad (9)$$

If the neural network has overlearned data the TRD error becomes small but the CHD error becomes large, so the smallest number of iterations I^s is the best.

- Step 6: This is the simplification of THEN with the backward elimination method. Among the m neural network input variables THEN for each inference rule, one input variable xp is arbitrarily eliminated and the NN of each part THEN is trained using TRD as step 6 Equation 10 gives the squared error of the control value. θ_{m-1}^{sp} of the control value. From the control value of the sth rule in the case of removing x^p This θ_{m-1}^{sp} can be estimated using the CHD

$$\theta_{m-1}^{sp} = \sum_{i=1}^{n_c} \{y_i - u_s(x_i) \cdot \mu_A^s(x_i)\}^2 \ , \ \text{p=1,2,...,m} \quad (10)$$

By comparison equations (8) and (10) it is

$$^s{}_m \Theta > \Theta^{sp}{}_{m-1}$$

The significance of the elimination of the input variables x can be considered minimal and x p can be neglected.

- Step 7: The same operations as in step 5 are carried out for input variables m-1. Steps 5 and 6 are repeated cyclically and in the next step of equation 6 would not hold for input variables. The model that gives the minimum value of O is the best NN. Therefore steps 1-7 determine the IF parts and THEN parts of each inference rule. Then the system identification process for the fuzzy model is completed.

- Step 8: The following equation can derive the final control value y :

$$y_i^* = \frac{\sum_{s=1}^{r} \mu_A^s(x_i) \cdot u_i(x_i)}{\sum_{s=1}^{r} \mu_A^s(x_i)} \ , \ \text{i=1,2,...,n.} \quad (11)$$

Where $u_s(x_i)$ is a value obtained when CHD is substituted into the best NN in step 7.

This method is used to determine the core boundaries by defining the boundary points to determine the core diameter for sorting.

4

Mathematical development and reasoning of the basis of the bioinformatics tool prototype

4.1 Overview:

In order to classify the image, it is first necessary to know how the image is constituted and how to work with it. For this, a *pipeline* is organised and the development begins.

As has been seen, the computer receives the information, from a camera that captures the image. The images to feed the model must be standardised and cleaned. Preprocessing allows the complexity to be reduced and the accuracy of the algorithm to be increased by making the images available for processing by a more general algorithm.

Each image is standardised through operations such as resizing, rotating, transforming it from one colour system to another or from colour to greyscale, defining an outline, etc. Only by standardising can it be properly compared; (pre-processing of data).

The features that are distinguishable from the *DNA* molecule in the comet test are then extracted and we must distinguish (bottom, head and tail). The result of this process is a feature vector, which is a list of unique shapes that identify the target object.

To see the behaviour of the functions, some tests were performed with the following classification simulator, seeing if it managed to classify, with how many epochs and loss test. The performance with sigmoid activation can be seen in Fig. 14 and with Tanh and Relu in Fig. 15.

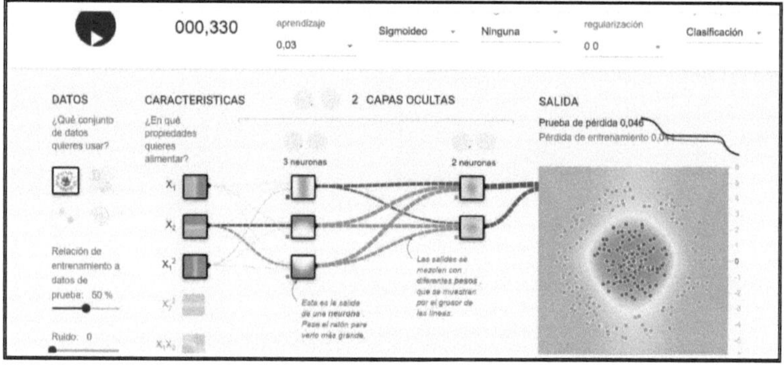

Figure 14Simulation of the model with sigmoid activation

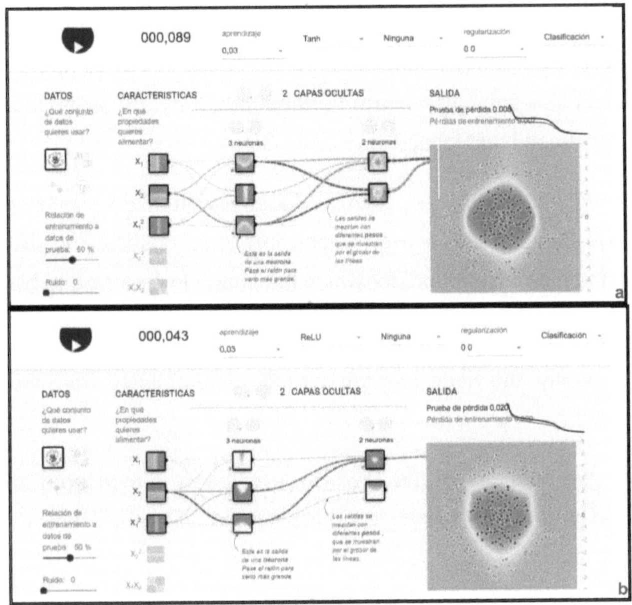

Figure 15Simulation with 2 hidden layers problem with activation a)RELU and activation b)Tanh using playgroundtensorflow neural network simulator .

With these characteristics, a classification model is created, using the sigmoid function fundamentally for its output range between 0 and 1. As can be seen in the simulated models, the activation with RELU and Tanh classify in fewer epochs and also offer lower values in the loss test. Although RELU is the most frequently used function in convolutional networks and is non-linear, sigmoidal activation is chosen because of the output range, which in this case study applies perfectly to the desired output and the times required for the extra epochs are absolutely negligible with current GPUs and TPUs.

This step analyses the feature vector and predicts the class to which the image belongs, which is the expertise of the geneticist.

In the prototype:

- First, the background is observed and distinguished from the *DNA* molecule and, if possible, the diameter of the nucleus is measured. For this, the images are first equalised with respect to light input and rotation in order to obtain equalised comparisons, or with a similar analysis environment. At this point we speak specifically about the imaging because the samples are prepared according to a strict procedure. Furthermore, they are saved in separate files to be processed by Matlab® and GNU Octave.

- The head and tail of the *DNA* nucleoid are then differentiated, *the* colour image is transformed to a grey tone image to observe the differences with respect to the background, for which the image is binarised to black and white to facilitate detection and measurement. The image becomes binary.

- Subsequently, the head and tail, already differentiated from the bottom, are measured.

- Finally, the diameter of the *DNA* nucleoid head is measured and compared with the tail measurement, establishing the different ratios defined in the classification model.

This process determines and classifies molecules into classes according to appropriately defined characteristics.

Although it can classify each class, the *test set* in the first prototype example yields a number of errors, as the algorithm is fine-tuned, it becomes more accurate. The main problem at this point, apart from correctly determining the thresholds, was finding a sufficient number of images. Such specific cytogenetic *datasets* are not found, because the preparation (specifically the fluorescence) is sensitive to light exposure, very few images are chosen for publication and even fewer are published. It was therefore a challenging finding.

The data bank of 200 images, composed of comet images recorded in the cytogenetics laboratory during a period of time from approximately 2009 to the present, where in the case of fish it refers to the species *Steindachnerina brevipinna (sabalito)*, *Piaractus mesopotamicus* (pacu) and in molluscs belong to the species *Corbicula fluminea* and *Limnoperna fortunei*. We worked with comet images from several species, because it is not possible to obtain enough images of samples from a single species to integrate the data set (*dataset*) with which the model is trained and validated. Although hundreds of preparations are studied in the laboratory, the photographic records are taken only from the best samples, since exposure to light erodes the fluorescence, the comet is extinguished and no further analysis is possible. Therefore, the best images from the photographic records remain for use by researchers in publications, posters and scientific journals. The training and testing of algorithms begins. By carrying out the classification tests, first with a training set of 78 very specific examples (the group of fish *Steindachnerina brevipinna* and *Piaractus mesopotamicus*), and then with images of bivalves, it is possible to consider and evaluate the performance of the model in the classification proposed by the prototype, and at the same time great flexibility in the presentation of *datasets* with new elements, including those of different species. In the laboratory we work with this technique applied to different biological models and within each biological model to different tissues, where each tissue and each animal (fish, mollusc, etc.) has its biological particularities, i.e. the cells are not the same, so the sizes of the comets and their morphology will not be the same either. For this reason, sufficient flexibility is also necessary.

When incorporating different images, more pre-processing must be done to clean up the images and extract features more easily. To achieve this, the images are scaled and transformed and saved in separate files to be later processed by Matlab® or Octave. This operation is also an added value as it allows a record and history of the classified samples to be kept.

In this step also, the program is initially adjusted many times, changing the classifier algorithm in Matlab®, as well as trying to find the most suitable threshold detection. In the research, Extreme Region Detection and Hough transform were tested, verifying the positions of the accumulator with the highest value, local maxima in the accumulator space. Matlab® uses *Houghpeack* to identify the peaks of the transform and *Houghlines* extracts the line segments based on the transform. Although we finally used *regionprops* which returns measurements for the set of properties specified for each object in the binary image, which can also work on the volumetric image with parameters for 3d and even return more statistics, and *struct array* which contains a structure for each object in the image. The first performance tests were done with a test set consisting of a few images 1 of each class in the beginning and then 1 of each validation class. Throughout the process the prototype was tested with 30 images, after the first tests, 48 more were tested and 122 images were validated. All tasks are added together to improve the performance of the model. In this prototype the tests managed to classify accurately, using simple functions as we will see below. The images go through processes to achieve their digital classification, resulting in a working prototype. The following steps were carried out in this process:

1. Input image selection.
2. Image pre-processing.
3. Feature extraction.
4. Classification.

In the process of image recognition, the fundamental phases are as follows:

- Extraction of features or characteristics of the physical system.
- Selection of characteristics.
- Obtaining the decision rule (classifier design).
- Use of the adaptive rule.

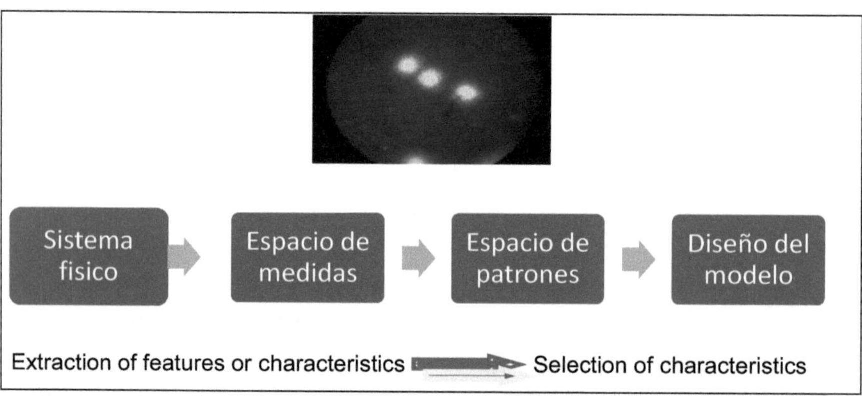

Figure 16Image of DNA molecule after Comet Assay preparation and model image pattern recognition strategy. Own source.

In the scheme of Fig16 the *pipeline* proposal is detailed, the samples of the medium are captured (Physical System), measured (Measurement Space) and transformed to a homogeneous image (Pattern Space), from where the descriptors of the chosen features are extracted to then go through a classifier developed from the features (Model Design). In other words, so that the process of the human eye distinguishing images and classifying them, can be done through a pattern recognition model of images, where the computer can see and through filters and models, recognise and classify the images imitating human behaviour (Fig.17).

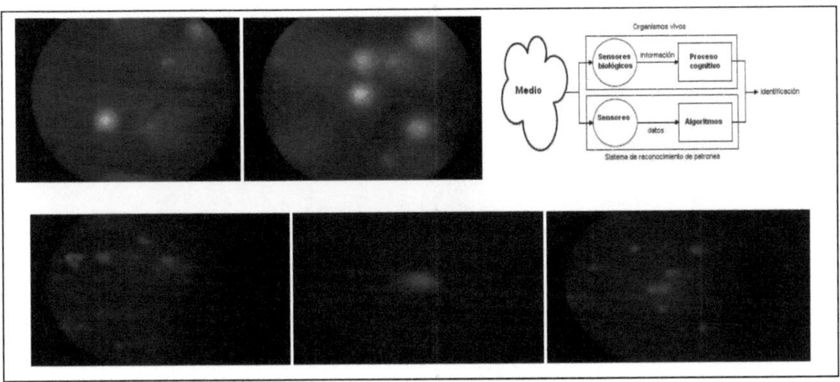

Figure 17Example of image pattern recognition; the raw image and transformed to achieve a uniform histogram. Own source.

For the development of the solution algorithm, different strategies were tested, applying the adaptive recognition strategy Fig18 to the case study, and the performance was measured between classes.

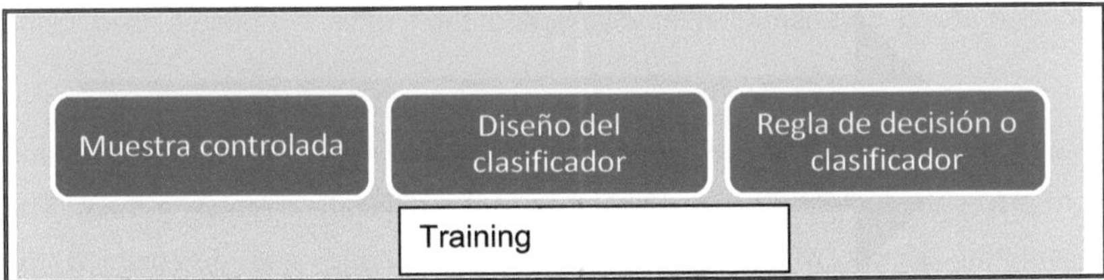

Figure 18Image path through the adaptive recognition training model for classification. Own source.

In our model we apply the adaptive recognition strategy where we first homogenise the data so that the treatment has the same base histogram as shown in Fig. 19.

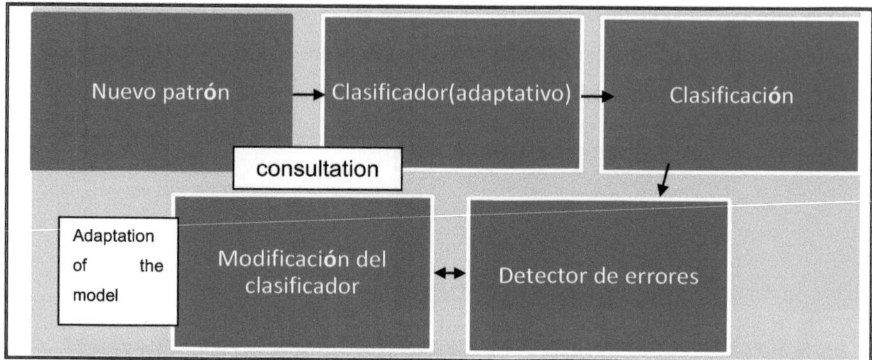

Figure 19Adaptation of the Model. Own source.

To carry out the diagnosis, detection and segmentation of the image of the *DNA* molecule as a whole is necessary. And regardless of the way the information is processed, it is difficult to find a method that is robust, accurate and yet flexible enough to adapt to the change in the samples.

First, the segmentation of the *DNA* molecule requires identifying the different components of the image, in our case study corresponding to the head, tail and bottom of the *DNA* nucleoid. To do this, a morphological decomposition of the image is performed using segmentation functions and then data is homogenised using filters.

The intensity and colour of the tail can be confused with the background and therefore errors in clustering are possible due to the difficulty in isolating them. The same problem occurs when defining the nucleoid head and determining the boundaries.

The challenge at this stage is to be flexible enough to determine the boundaries of the nucleoid head while using the same rules to measure all DNA nucleoid heads, or the same decision system to determine in the image the region where the nucleoid head, tail and background are observed and what their boundaries are (Fig. 20). The nucleoid is the brightest part in the centre, followed by the tail, which is the brightest and dimmest part, and everything else in the background, although sometimes more than one nucleoid is present in the image.

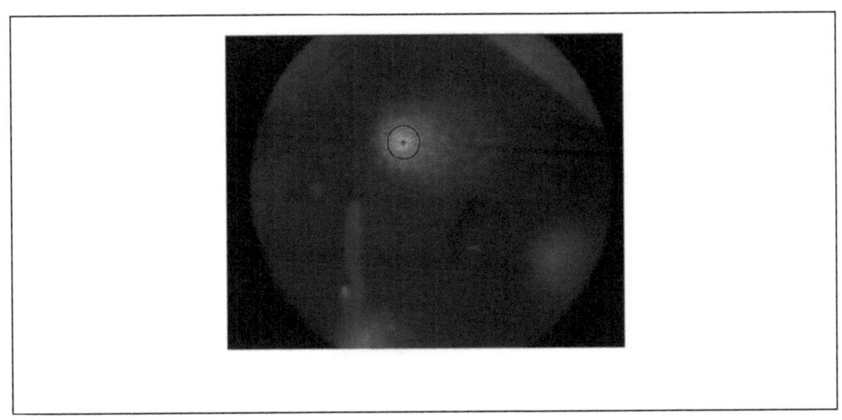

Figure 20First approximation of detection of DNA nuclei or nucleoids. The complexity of defining the boundaries can be seen.

Finally, although the samples follow the same protocol of preparation of the biological material, in the experimental treatment, the images are not always homogeneous. Images from the photographic recording of phenotypically different cells, which even appear different, may belong to the same class. (Fig. 21).

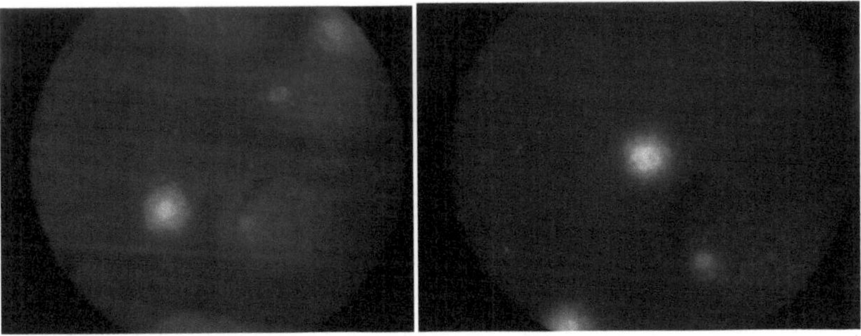

Figure 21Note two images of Comet belonging to the same class.

The segmentation of the nucleoid head of the DNA molecule is performed in different steps, first the head and tail are detected and located, then delimited and measured.

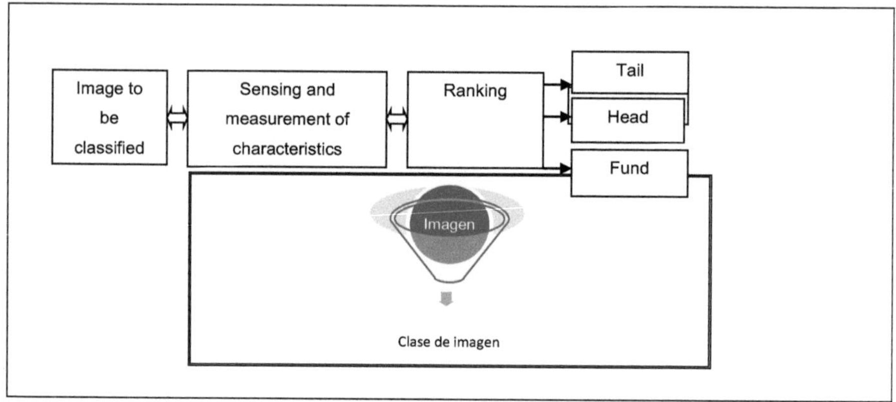

Figure 22Classification according to morphological composition with respect to the model.   Own source

The procedure begins with obtaining the photograph, fig. 23, from which the pattern recognition design had to solve the following:

- Pre-processing or feature selection problems.
- Problems of calculation or measurement of characteristics.
- Identification and classification or grouping problems.

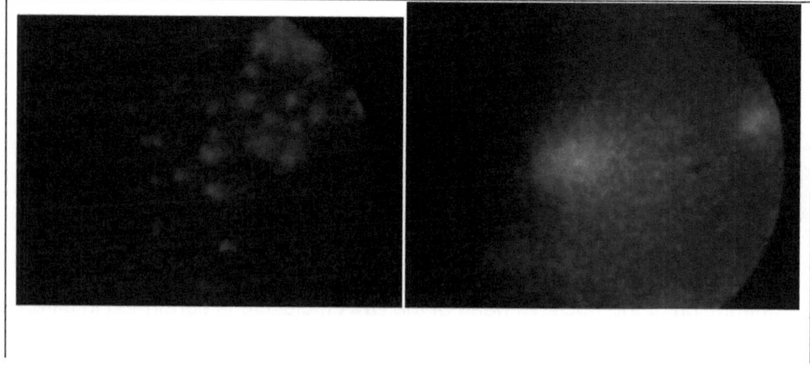

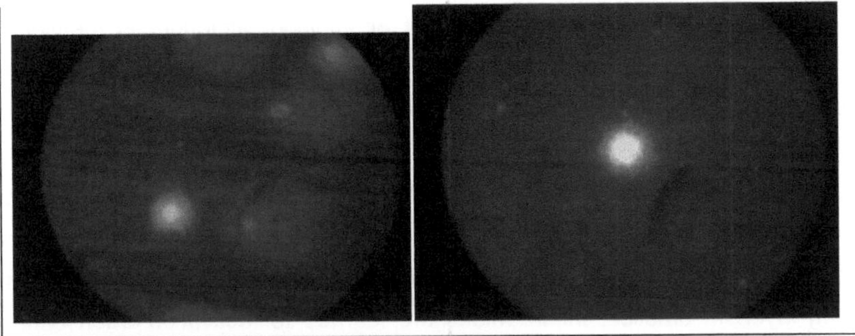

Figure 23Different photographs of DNA nucleoids before pre-processing. They show differences not only in the number of nucleoids but also in light and position.

4.2 Mathematical development of the predicate

Representation primitive:

The representation primitive is the pixel. The discrete representation (digital image) is an approximation, given a finite number of samples. The pixel represents light intensity in grey levels, and can represent any physical, chemical or biological quantity.

The image to be classified falls into multi-level images, L grey levels usually L=256. U L grey level images (scalar).

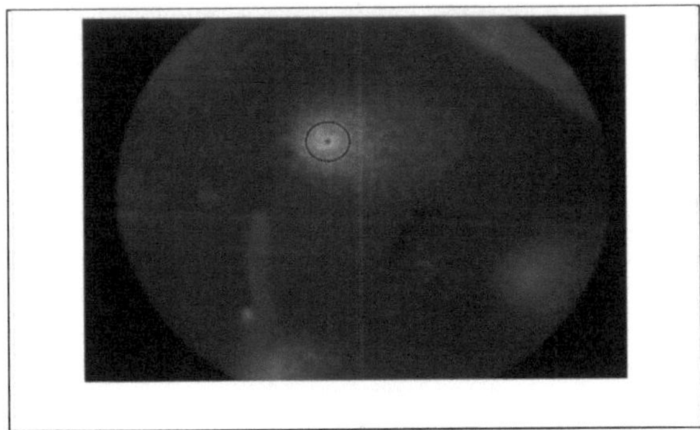

Figure 24 Measurement of the comet nucleus before transforming to grey levels. Photograph taken from the programme after determining the centroid Own source.

As can be seen in Fig. 24 before the transformations it is very difficult to determine the boundary or limits even though at first glance it would seem simple. The boundary depends very much on judgement or intuition, although as mentioned before in this case study functions were used to determine the regions and thresholds. Grey-scale transformation is also used as part of the preprocessing.

The input layer takes the values of all pixels. Moving to the hidden layer extracts the features of an image, and performs two main operations, grouping and the definition of a set of trainable filters that process the image together with the values of the preceding layer. In practice, these values are learned for activation when certain features are found. If they are cascaded, different degrees of abstraction or depth are obtained. In other words, these filters return the features that are evaluated in an image and each pass of each filter takes some of them, which is why this stage is so important. Then through clustering an even smaller matrix is made, so that the number of connections is sufficiently manageable.

Filtering in the spatial domain: linear filters based on convolution masks

A convolution filter can be represented as a square or rectangular matrix (convolution matrix) of much smaller dimensions than the image on which it will be applied. This matrix is shifted over the image so that the central element of the matrix coincides with each of the pixels in the image as shown in Fig. 25, defining the pixel for example as $p(x)$=pixel is dark grey.

At each position, the value of each image pixel is multiplied by the value of the position of the matrix element. The image pixel that coincides with the central element of the matrix is then replaced by the sum of the products. Subsequently, the clustering is performed and the convolution layer is obtained, and the layer of interleaved clusters, as many times as we have filters. The main characteristics in the segmentation process are: colour, shape and grey intensity or black and white distinction in our case.

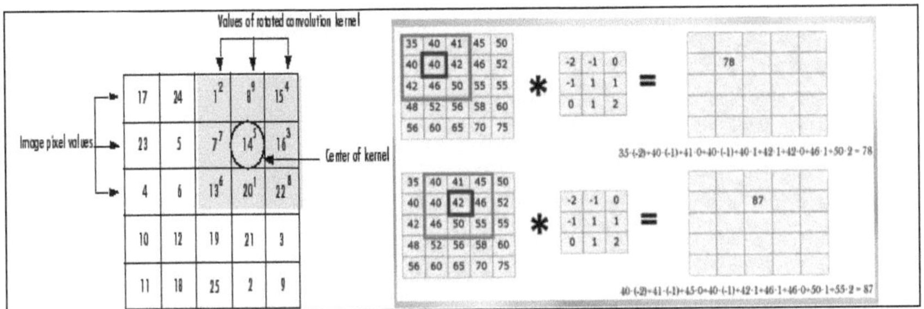

Figure 25How the convolution matrix traverses the image.

4.3 Classifier

Data: Characteristics that allow membership of the class. From an experimental treatment of 10-15 individuals per treatment, 100 cells per individual are counted and sorted according to the length and intensity of the comet tails, which are equivalent to fragmented or damaged *DNA*.

Individual to be classified: it appears in the photographs as a comet, with a clearer nucleus and a halo around it, of different shapes according to the *DNA* damage (as we will see later) that will determine the class to which it belongs. The very disintegrated halo belongs to class 4, which includes the anomalous ones.

Classes:

Class 0 = no tail, only head or core (no damage) Fig. 26

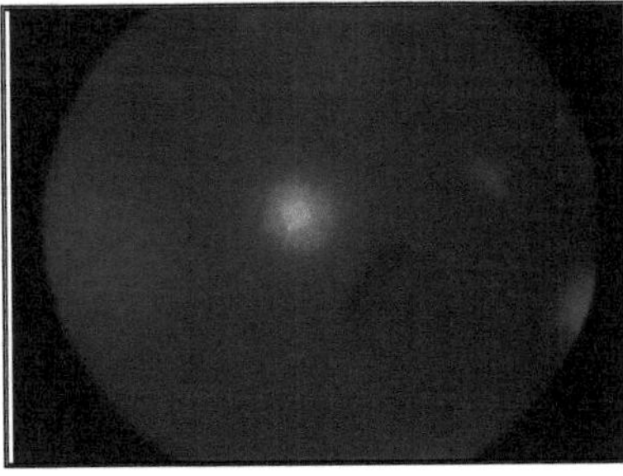

Figure 26The individual to be classified appears as a comet without a tail. The nucleus is very bright, the tail around it is less bright and the background is orange.

Class 1 = tail size up to one times the diameter of the head Fig.27

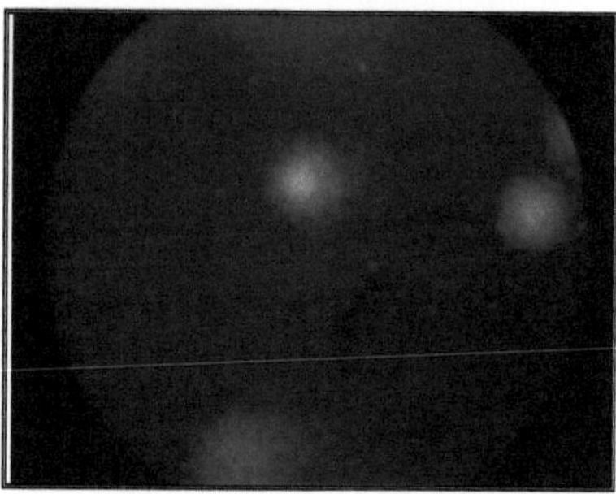

Figure 27Class 1 image, the nuclei can be seen with a lighter colour and the tail is the size of the diameter of the head.

Class 2 = tail size up to twice the diameter of the head Fig. 28

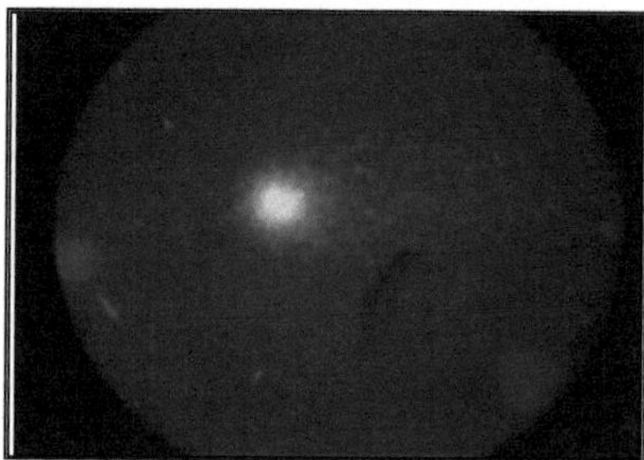

Figure 28Tail extends more than twice the diameter of the nucleoid.

Class 3 = tail size up to three times the diameter of the head Fig. 29

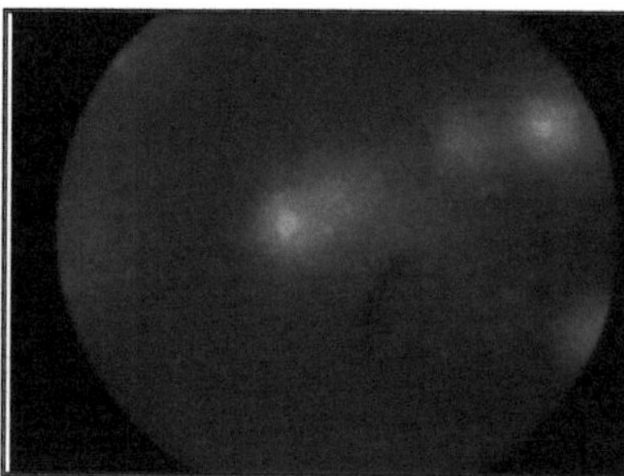

Figure 29Class 3 image shows the tail extending 3 times the diameter of the nucleoid.

Class 4 = almost all DNA is fragmented, this group includes abnormal Fig. 30.

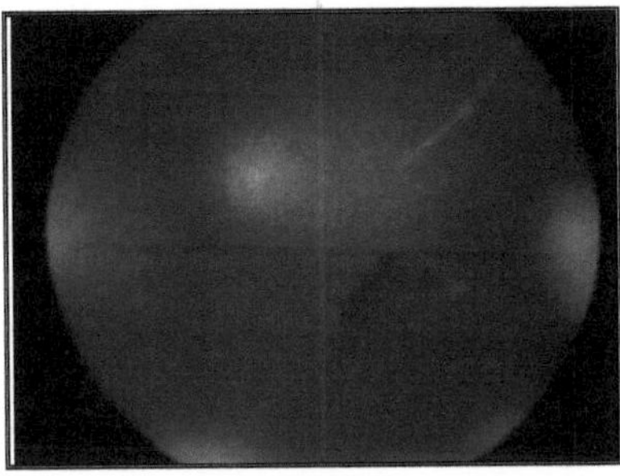

Figure 30Class 4 image shows the nucleus and the largely disintegrated tail.

Objective: to classify each *DNA* molecule within the class or category to which it belongs Fig. 31.

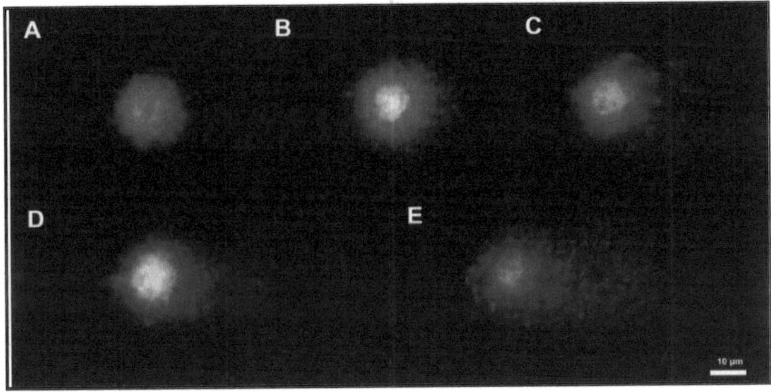

Figure 31Sample of the different classes of comets. The letters A,B,C,D,E correspond to classes 0, class 1, class 2, class 3 and class 4 where the anomalous ones are also found. **Source: Edited photograph Cytogenetics Laboratory (UNaM-IBS-CONICET).**

The process is: when viewing an image, the prototype is able to classify it and has sufficient flexibility in distinguishing the tail from the background through fuzzy logic algorithms.

From the classification we obtain the class memberships shown in Fig. 31. Supervised learning algorithms are also used with reference to Fig. 32 for error handling and learning.

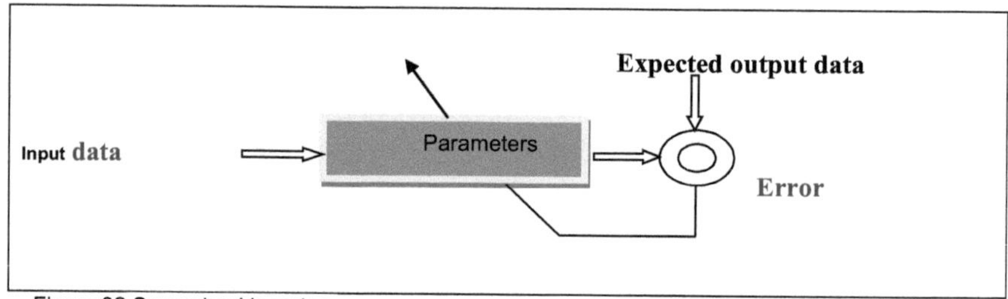

Figure 32 Supervised learning.

4.4 Grouping or classification

The convolution matrix can be used to work with different filters, for example:

Focus, Blur, Edge Enhancement, Edge Detection, Sobel Filter, Sharpen Filter, and achieve a feature vector (Fig.33). In Matlab® the default Sobel filter BW=edge(I) returns a binary image containing s where the function finds edges in the input image and s elsewhere. By default, BW uses the Sobel edge detection method, which finds edges at those points where the image gradient is maximal, using the Sobel approximation to the derivative. With the "log" method it finds edges by looking for zero crossings after filtering with a Laplacian of Gaussian (LoG) filter.

For gradient magnitude edge detection methods (Sobel, Prewitt, Roberts), the **calculated** gradient magnitude.**edgethreshold** is used as the threshold.

For zero-crossing methods, including Gaussian Laplacian, **zero.edgethreshold** is used as the threshold for **zero** crossings. In other words, a large jump through zero is an edge, while a small jump is not.

The Canny method applies two thresholds to the gradient: a high threshold for low edge sensitivity and a low threshold for high edge sensitivity. It starts with the low sensitivity result and then grows it to include connected edge pixels from the high **sensitivity** result.**edge** This helps to fill gaps in the detected edges. However, in the developed algorithm **Imclose** was used to fill the gaps in the edges.

In all cases, it chooses the default threshold heuristically, depending on the **input** data.**edge**. The best way to vary the threshold is to run once, capturing the calculated threshold as the second **output** argument.**edge** Then, from the value calculated by setting the threshold higher to detect fewer edge pixels or lower to detect more **edge** pixels.**edge**.

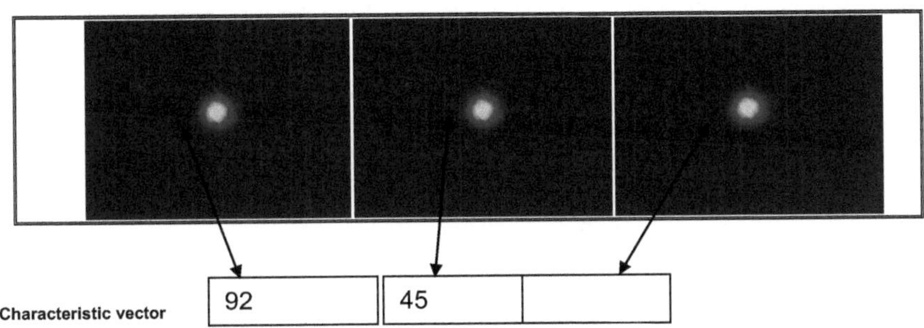

Figure 33 Example of the use of a multiresolution feature vector .

After applying the filters through functions in this case, both the head of *DNA* nucleoids (the centre of the centroid is determined and a line is drawn to determine the diameter, sine and cosine functions are also used to determine the coordinates) is easily measured, the nucleoid is then measured and as a difference with respect to the head, the tail is obtained, and can also be clearly differentiated from the background by binarisation. The raw photograph Fig34 can be seen before pre-processing.

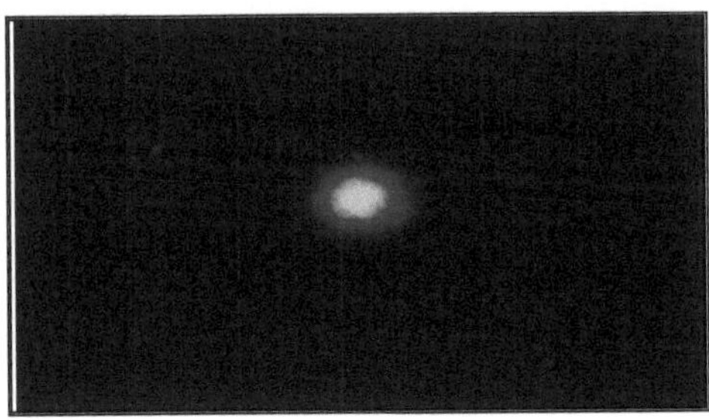

Figure 34Photograph taken under the microscope in total darkness. Raw image. Own source.

By changing the colour scale to grey, we can observe more clearly the different aspects of the *DNA* nucleoid and differentiate its morphological characteristics, separate the head and tail by separating it from the background, and then differentiate the tail from the background and distinguish the nucleoid head from the tail in order to start the classification process. To do this, we perform a series of operations such as, for example:

- Transfer function for contrast enhancement

This function is applied to switch to greyscale and then the functions are applied to determine the threshold as explained above. It clearly shows the different features that we need to isolate in order to measure and classify.

$$\mu_{out} = T(\mu_{in}) = \begin{cases} 0 & \mu_{in} \leq \mu_1 \\ 2.5 \,(\mu_{in} - \mu_1) & \mu_1 \leq \mu_{in} < \mu_i \\ 255 & \mu_2 \mu_{in} \end{cases}$$

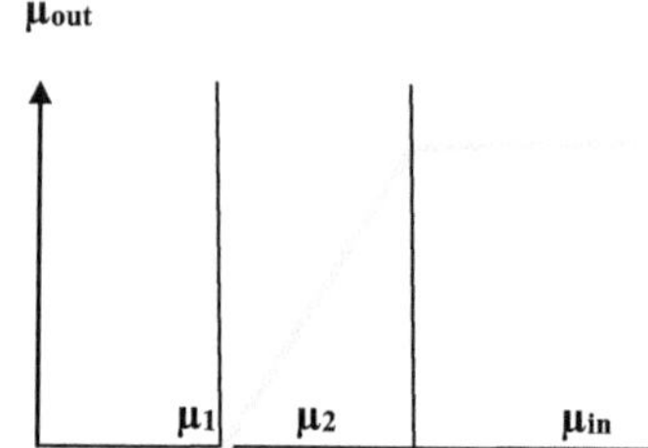

4.5 Contrast enhancement

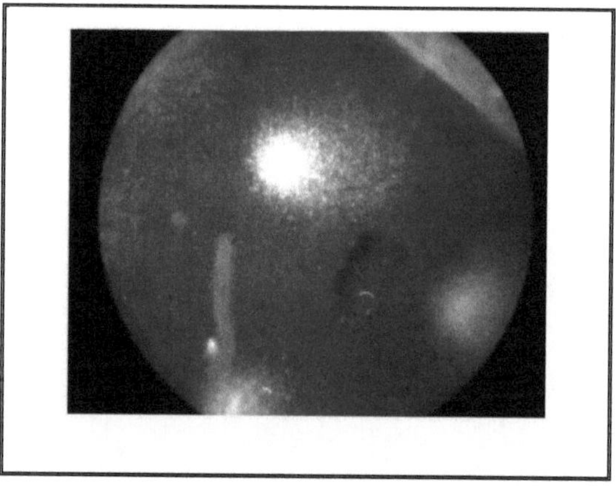

Figure 35Image after pre-processing (image prepared in greyscale). Source: image modified from a photograph taken at the Cytogenetics Laboratory (UNaM-IBS-CONICET) as a result of the algorithm developed.

This image is a product of the **IMADJUST** function in Matlab®, which allows us to achieve a similar histogram, as we can see in Fig. 35. This function makes the lights and shadows standardised and by homogenising the image, with the same light and shadow parameters, an equalised histogram is achieved to analyse each image and thus classify it.

This function is very important because in biological material, the *DNA* nucleoids, as we saw earlier in the photos, the images of the object of study can appear rotated, overlapping or with more light or shadow depending on where they are in the sample: even though the samples are prepared so that the tails migrate to the same side.

Fig. 36 shows how the image is brought to binary, black and white. The threshold is set through the **regionprop** function in BW = imread ('text.png');

which determines the centroid and position of the object of study, and establishes regions after filling in the gaps by making the border solid through **Imclose**. The image with the superimposed centroids can be observed through the function: imshow(BW) hold on plot(centroids(:,1),centroids(:,2),'b*') hold off.

This process allows us to establish head and tail clearly, although the image still has some porosity with blank spaces generated by the biological material.

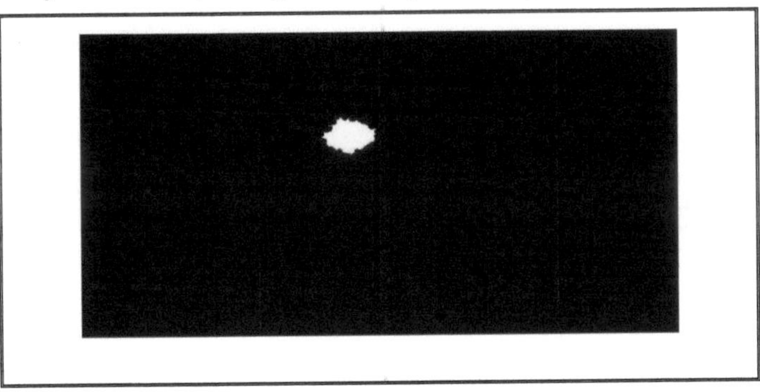

Figure 36Binary image (black and white) of the DNA molecule after applying the Imclose function.

Then, through the IMCLOSE function, these blanks or pores are filled in until a solid image is achieved, which allows us to define the boundary and automatically determine the limit through some mathematical operations. The interesting thing in this part of the process is to find the right value for the closure of the figure.

After this transformation of the image, it is easier to perform the operations by defining borders. The centre is calculated by establishing two diameter measurements. A centroid is defined (length and width are measured) through the functions mentioned above and a line is drawn by measuring the diameter as shown in Fig. 37.

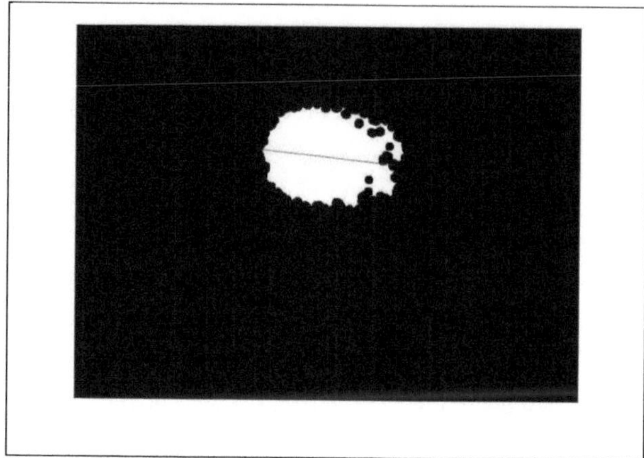

Figure 37Binary image of the cell. You can also see the line defined by the algorithm measuring the diameter of the nucleoid plus the tail.

4.6 Classifier code for Matlab® and Octave

In the code of the classifier prototype, the functions described above are commented out:

```
clc
clear all
I=imread('P1010174.jpg');
S = sum(I,3);
meanI= max(S(:)) %meanI=mean2(I)
Load the images
A = im2bw(I,0.53);
se = strel('disk',5);
A = imclose(A,se);
B = im2bw(I,0.41);
se = strel('disk',13);
B = imclose(B,se);
```

```matlab
% Find the difference of the images
closeBW=B-A;
figure
% Defines the borders of the two images.
dim = size(A);
col = round(dim(2)/2)-90;
row = min(find(A(:,col)));
boundary1 = bwtraceboundary(A,[row, col],'N');
dim = size(B);
col = round(dim(2)/2)-90;
row = min(find(B(::,col)));
boundary2 = bwtraceboundary(B,[row, col],'N');


% Find the centre of the core
rx=mean(boundary1(:,2));
ry=mean(boundary1(:,1));


numofel=numel(boundary2(:,1));
maxx=0;
for i=1:numofel
    if sqrt((boundary2(i,2)-rx)^2+(boundary2(i,1)-ry)^2)> maxx
        maxx=sqrt((boundary2(i,2)-rx)^2+(boundary2(i,1)-ry)^2);
        Mx=boundary2(i,2);
        My=boundary2(i,1);
    end
end


minn=99999999;
for i=1:numofel
```

```matlab
        if sqrt((boundary2(i,2)-rx)^2+(boundary2(i,1)-ry)^2)< minn
            minn=sqrt((boundary2(i,2)-rx)^2+(boundary2(i,1)-ry)^2);
            mx=boundary2(i,2);
            my=boundary2(i,1);
        end
    end
end


%Displays the results
imshow(I)
hold on;
plot(boundary1(:,2),boundary1(:,1),boundary2(:,2),boundary2(:,1),'g','LineWidth',1);
plot(rx,ry,'*b')
plot(Mx,My,'*b')
plot(mx,my,'*b')


maxx
minn


```

Algorithm 2

```matlab
lc
clear all


Comment on this line to run in Matlab
pkg load image


Load the image
```

```matlab
prompt = 'Enter filename:';

iname = input(prompt)

I=imread(iname);

res=size(I(:,:,1)); %Determines the resolution of the input image

grayI=rgb2gray(I);

grayI=imadjust(grayI);

%A = im2bw(I,double(max(grayI(:)))/422); %Puts the kernel image in black and white

A = im2bw(I,0.53); %Passes to black and white the image of the nucleus

se = strel('disk',round(mean(res(:))/200),0);

A = imclose(A,se); %Close holes in the kernel image

CCA = bwconncomp(A,8); %Detect connected objects from the kernel image

SA = regionprops(CCA, 'Area');

L = labelmatrix(CCA);

A = ismember(L, find([SA.Area] >= 0.6*max([SA.Area]))); %Delete all objects 40% smaller
than the largest object

SA = regionprops(A, 'Centroid','MajorAxisLength','MinorAxisLength');

centroidA = cat(1,SA.Centroid);

radiiA=mean([SA.MajorAxisLength SA.MinorAxisLength],2)/2;

figure(1);

imshow(A);


Repeats the same operations for the queue
%B = im2bw(I,mean(grayI(:))/104);

B = im2bw(I,0.30);

se = strel('disk',round(mean(res(:))/100),0);

B = imclose(B,se);
```

```matlab
CCB = bwconncomp(B,8);

SB = regionprops(CCB, 'Area');

L = labelmatrix(CCB);

B = ismember(L, find([SB.Area] >= 0.6*max([SB.Area])));

SB = regionprops(B, 'Centroid','MajorAxisLength','Orientation');

centroidB = cat(1,SB.Centroid);

figure(2);

imshow(B);


Draws a line through the centroid

hlen = SB.MajorAxisLength/2;

xCentre = SB.Centroid(1);

yCentre = SB.Centroid(2);

cosOrient = cosd(SB.Orientation);

sinOrient = sind(SB.Orientation);

xcoords = xCentre + hlen * [cosOrient -cosOrient];

ycoords = yCentre + hlen * [-sinOrient sinOrient];

line(xcoords, ycoords);

rela=99;

figure(3);

imshow(I);

hold on;

if sum(centresA(:))>0

    plot(centresA(:,1),centresA(:,2),'b*');

    viscircles(centresA,radiiA,'Colour','b');
```

```matlab
    distR=sqrt((centresA(:,1)-centresB(:,1))^2+(centresA(:,2)-centresB(:,2))^2);

    Calculates the ratio of tail to diameter.

    rela=(hlen+distR-radiosA)/(2*radiosA)
end


plot(centresB(:,1),centresB(:,2),'r*');
plot(xCentre ,yCentre, xcoords, ycoords );
hold off;
if rela<=0.5
    disp("Class 0")
  end
if rela>0.5 & rela<=1
    disp("Class 1")
  end
if rela>1 & rela<=2
    disp("Class 2")
  end
if rela>2 & rela<=3
   disp("Class 3")
  end
if rela>3
    disp("Class 4")
end
%Displays the results
```

```matlab
hold on;

figure(4);

imshow(grayI);
```

5

Results and discussion

5.1 Results

This master thesis substantiates scientific developments in the broad field of biological image processing, in particular in the recognition and classification of images obtained with epifluorescence microscopy and classified by means of the Comet Assay technique.

Most of the processes involving signals, in which biological material is involved, bring with them a great difficulty in handling the data (noise, capture, non-uniformity of data, variations of the biological material, among others). Another complicated aspect of handling biological data is the extraction of its characteristics, mainly due to the differences between one class and another, and even when analysing data from the same sample. The same sample may have different light focuses or even several overlapping cells. Therefore, equalisation becomes relevant, or in other words, it provides a level playing field for the analysis of the samples by offering an even histogram. In order to achieve these unique characteristics in each sample, a series of processes, mathematical functions, filters and algorithms are used to achieve this equalisation.

Algorithms for parameter detection of these images must incorporate aspects of generalisation that involve pre-processing to achieve the generality sought. This point, in the case study, could have been a challenge as there were several different species to classify.

Classifying images is also a complicated task, if the detection of the parameters that have been selected as significant is not adequate.

These processes are carried out with real images of real samples that involve mathematical and computational algorithms to obtain results. The results obtained in the processes developed here predispose us to continue with research in this branch of Biomedical Engineering and also to continue along the path of data sciences, positioning these processes as a support for the specialist's decision-making.

Various signal processing techniques have been presented from the theoretical framework. By exploiting an adaptive approach, it is possible to improve the performance of these processing systems, relative to classical strategies. Through the techniques addressed in this research, typical problems of object recognition in images can be successfully addressed, i.e., invariance to object geometric distortions, background noise, sensor noise and non-homogeneous illumination is provided in terms of their discrimination capability and computational complexity.

The topics developed in the research work are interrelated, so that some serve as pre-processing for others, or post-processing, as in the case of the application of mathematical algorithms for adjusting the weights of neural networks.

The computational intelligence methodology best suited to the case is a neuro-fuzzy hybrid, since, as discussed above, biological samples do not fit exactly into each defined class but sometimes there are fuzzy areas where fuzzy methods have to be considered (e.g. an active threshold). Nevertheless, an adequate classification is achieved with simple functional procedures, as mentioned above. In the case study, classification is achieved very accurately, because the algorithm is developed in Matlab® specifically for this case.

In this case, the development of the functional prototype is done in Matlab® and can be executed in GNU Octave. The possibility of running the algorithms in GNU Octave is what makes it possible to move forward with the prototype.

One of the proposals for the future includes the creation of an application that incorporates the prototype procedure into a smartphone equipped with special filters to treat fluorescence. This proposal would not reduce technology (since the laboratory has special microscopes on which the camera is supported to take photographs of the samples), but would replace the digital camera by incorporating new technology that would also allow more convenient management of storage, classification and counting.

Matlab® has a module that allows the algorithm to be compiled into an app that can be run on a mobile phone. Running the software also optimises sample sorting times.

With this, it is proposed to expand the range of solutions for different possible cases in the laboratory and thus find, from a variety of solutions, the method that provides the best performance in classification and the most economically convenient resources when evaluating the implementation in the Cytogenetics laboratory (UNaM-IBS-CONICET). For the laboratory it is a genuine contribution that would greatly simplify research/classification times: it would also be an educational contribution specifically in the ecotoxicological genetics subject that corresponds to the higher cycle of orientation and regional flexibilisation of the degree in genetics of the new UNaM 2017 syllabus.

Throughout the final master's thesis, different tools for digital image processing are presented, in particular for images obtained with fluorescence microscopy using the Comet Assay technique.

The digital processing techniques used in this development incorporate the innovation of their application to the images obtained.

The use of hybrid Neuro Fuzzy and Somm algorithms with genetic algorithms were also presented as background to the research lines, including their conceptual bases carefully studied and presented for their application to the case. Preliminary results were presented in:

- WICC 2018 (Computer Science Workshop held at UNNE Ctes.).
  Vera Laceiras M. Silvia and Caffetti Yanina; "*Pattern recognition of digital images obtained by microscopy and parameterized according to the Micronucleus technique and the Comet Assay Technique used by the Laboratory of General Cytogenetics and Environmental Monitoring UNaM-IBS CONICET for the detection of cell damage.* "26 and 27 April 2018 Red UNCI - UNNE - ISBN 978-987-3619-27-4 Editorial Universidad Nacional del Nordeste (UNNE) 2018. Red de Universidades con Carreras en Informática (RedUNCI). http://sedici.unlp.edu.ar/handle/10915/69205 [50].

- And at the First International Congress on Science, Design and Technology (UNAE 2019).

  Vera Laceiras M. Silvia and Caffetti Yanina; "*Pattern recognition of digital images obtained by microscopy and parameterized according to the Micronucleus technique and the Comet Assay Technique used by the Laboratory of General Cytogenetics and Environmental Monitoring UNaM-IBS CONICET for the detection of cell damage*". October 1 and 2, 2019 With Publication in the academic and scientific University SAETA of the documentation centre of the Autonomous University of Encarnación ISSN: 2414 2506. https://www.unae.edu.py/tv/images/Memoria-del-I-Congreso-Internacional-de-ciencia-diseno-tecnologia-UNAE-2019.pdf [51].

- WICC 2020 (Computer Science Workshop developed virtually by the pandemic).

  Vera Laceiras M. Silvia; *"Digital processing of cytogenetic images for their classification according to the comet assay technique for the detection of DNA damage"*. Red UNCI - UNNE - article 12770 belonging to the area "Intelligent Agents and Systems". https://wicc2020.unpa.edu.ar/ [52].

For the pre-processing of the images, the images were processed by changing to greyscales and then binarised, segmented and stored in separate files to be analysed with Matlab® and Octave (Fig 38).

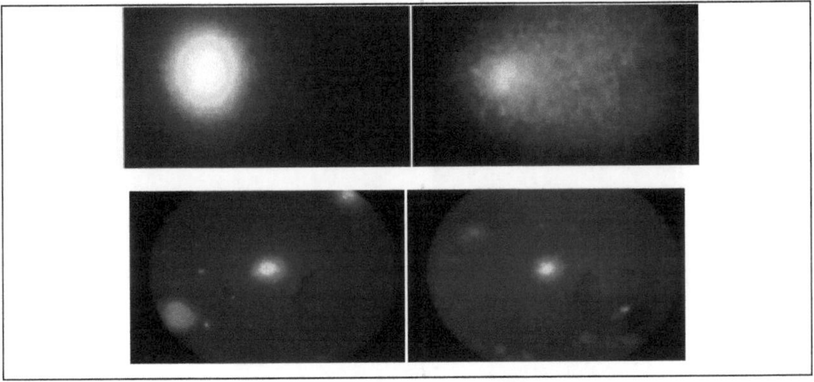

Figure 38Images of *DNA* nucleoids images obtained from the photographs.

Then the tilt of some images is detected and gently corrected so that the highlights and shadows generate an equalised histogram (Fig. 39).

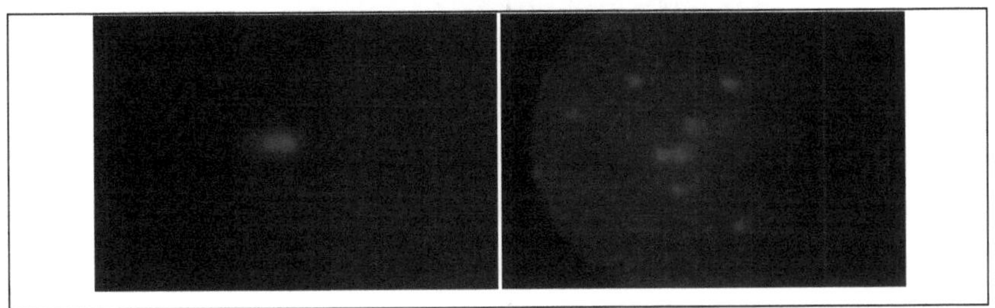

Figure 39DNA nucleoid images with pre-processing we obtain equalised images.

For this, different techniques are used such as colour changes through filters and grey scale, determination of the nucleoid centre, determination of coordinates and position through functions such as sine, cosine, ismember, streal among others (Fig.40) and the vector assembly through mathematical and computational algorithms. These functions make it possible to have suitable images for the detection and measurement of the descriptors of the images and their subsequent classification into the different Classes (Fig. 41).

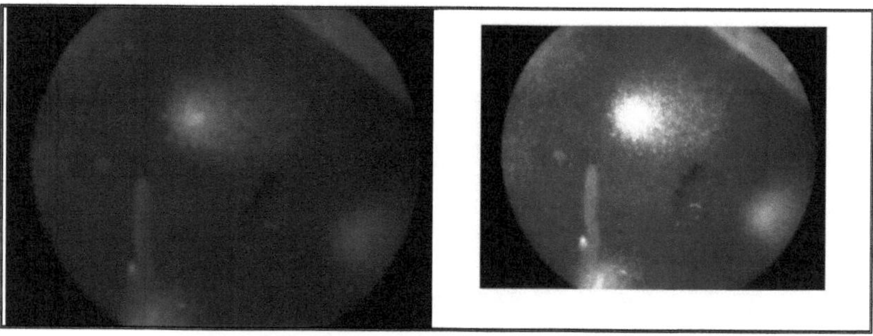

Figure 40DNA nucleoid images before and after transformation are shown in grayscale.

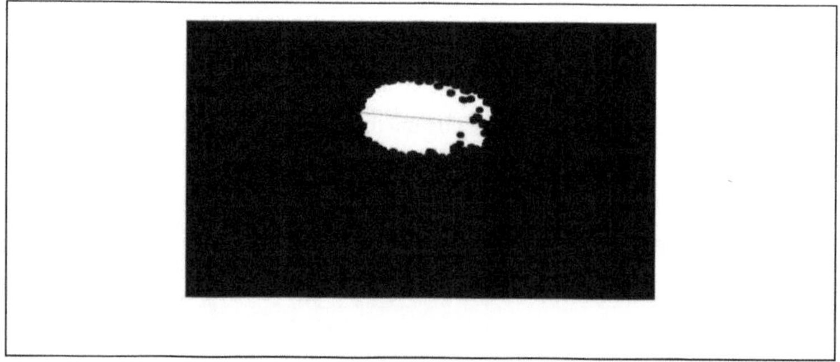

Figure 41Head and tail images of the nucleoid in black and white (binary).

The algorithm developed is based on image processing and artificial vision, where segmentation is of special relevance, in order to measure and differentiate the parts as a process prior to classification.

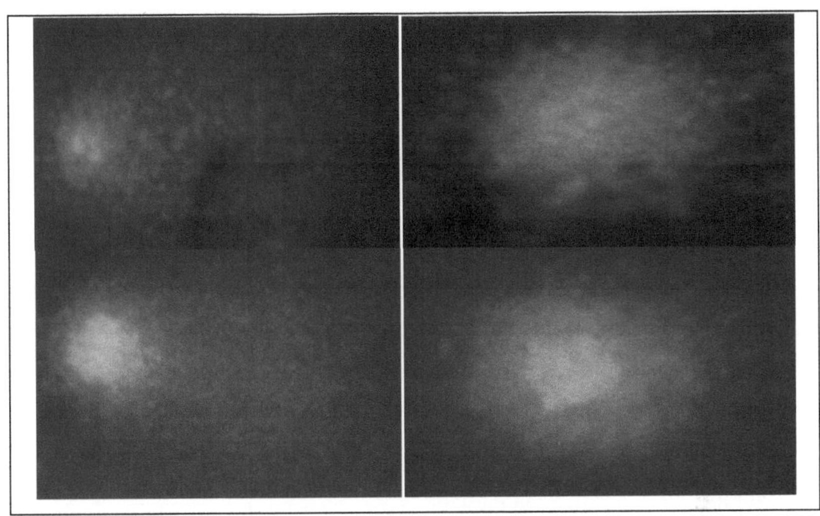

Figure 42 Images of biological material can look very different and yet belong to the same class.

Taking into account that the image being analysed is biological material (the limit of belonging to the different classes is not always clear) (Fig.42), we opted for the adaptation of neuro-fuzzy algorithms, so that membership of a certain class can be achieved through rules that allow flexibility, as very specific patterns lead to minimising the error in this specificity but increase the percentage of error in the generality. In the case study, having a dataset with few images, it is easy to fall into specificity. At the same time, it was necessary to find the defuzzification point that allows to determine up to where the head of the comet is considered, where the tail is considered and what percentage of the image belongs to the background. For this purpose, functions are used, as we have seen, to determine the regions and thresholds. The classifier algorithm (prototype) developed in MATLAB® and OCTAVE allows a sample to be entered and through functions such as **Imadjust** and others that determine the coordinates of the object or produce transformations, perform the classification almost without error, however it cannot be said that it really does a training, but rather the testing phase was rather to determine the active threshold and there is enough flexibility to then generalise.

As an example, a sample representing an anomaly (class 4) is shown (Fig. 43).

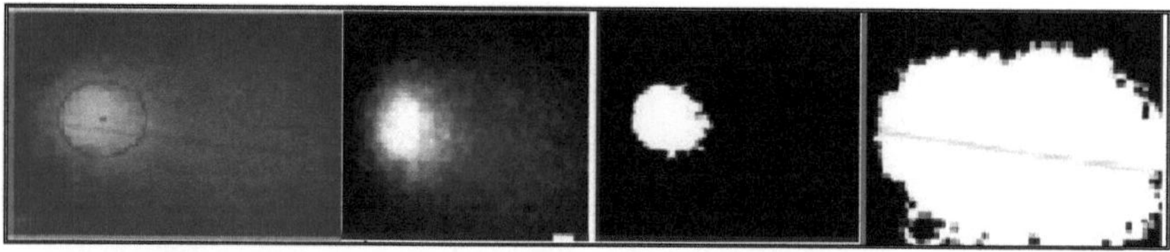

Figure 43 Classification of a photographic record of a sample belonging to an anomalous. Perform the same procedure and classify it as class 4.

The network is designed taking into account these fuzzy learning rules, widely spread not only in scientific developments but also in industry, but within the model as seen in the algorithm, no pre-trained Inception-v3, Inception-v5 or Convnet layered networks are used, but the algorithm is developed specifically for the data set of the case study.

These hybrids of intelligent computing allow decision management in areas of uncertainty, where linguistics is of interest and boundaries have no defined edges.

Finally, in the digital processing for image pattern classification, not only ocular inspection was performed on the image samples but also quantitative indices were found to support this visual assessment. The study and application of neural networks governed by heuristics define the network structure and inputs based on their morphological characteristics.

Based on the above, this final master's thesis demonstrates the applicability of these mathematical and computational algorithms presented through models or algorithms adapted to solve specific cases, as in this case study research, to make decisions in the classification of cytogenetic microscopic samples.

The design of the prototype tool with artificial intelligence concepts, machine learning and its implementation through simple functions, allows working with the cytogenetic images in the Comet assay.

Compared to what was being done before (classification by visual inspection), this variant allows effective classification results to be obtained, without having to keep an eye on the programming of the algorithms when the sample changes, and to obtain statistics that can be adjusted and rectified if necessary.

In the course of this final work, we obtained the following results:

The final performance of the system is assessed by visual inspection and data cross-validation methods. Using K (K-Fold) groups of data in which different types of classes and different species are represented in each group. In (K-Fold) where K represents the interactions, the error is calculated as follows:

$$Ei = \frac{numero\ de\ clasificaciones\ incorrectas}{total\ de\ datos\ del\ grupo\ test} \tag{12}$$

The final validation error is:

$$Error = \frac{1}{K}\sum_{i=1}^{k} E_i \tag{13}$$

The following average error is obtained: **Error 7.4%** conformed as follows in terms of precision, Table (3):

Table 3 Table of precision errors in each class.

Class	Accuracy Error
Class 0	0,00%
Class 1	8.18%
Class 2	14.3%
Class 3	14,00%
Class 4	6.2%

By measuring the accuracy of the classifications and according to the samples submitted, the following tables of accuracy and completeness were obtained (Tables 4 and 5).

Table 4 Accuracy Table

Class	Accuracy
Class 0	100,0%
Class 1	91,8%
Class 2	85,7%
Class 3	42,0%
Class 4	93,8%

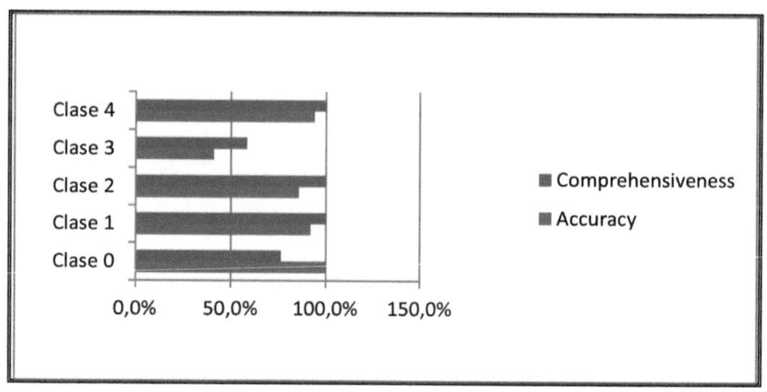

Figure 44Accuracy graph by class

Table 5 completeness table

Class	Comprehensiveness
Class 0	76,5%
Class 1	100,0%
Class 2	100,0%
Class 3	58,3%
Class 4	100,0%

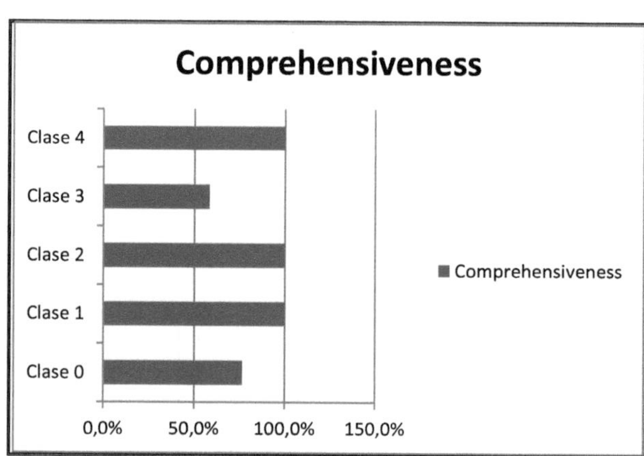

Figure 45Exhaustiveness chart by class.

Nevertheless, through well-defined functionality and a proper analysis of feature descriptors, together with mathematical algorithms, the expected classification results are achieved with relatively simple algorithms (Fig. 44 and 45). The confusion matrix is thus represented with the success cases (Table 6: Fig. 46):

Table 6 Confusion matrix

Confusion matrix	Class 0	Class 1	Class 2	Class 3	Class 4
Class 0		0	0	0	0
Class 1		45	0	0	0
Class 2	0	0		0	
Class 3	0	0	0	30	
Class 4	0	0	0	0	

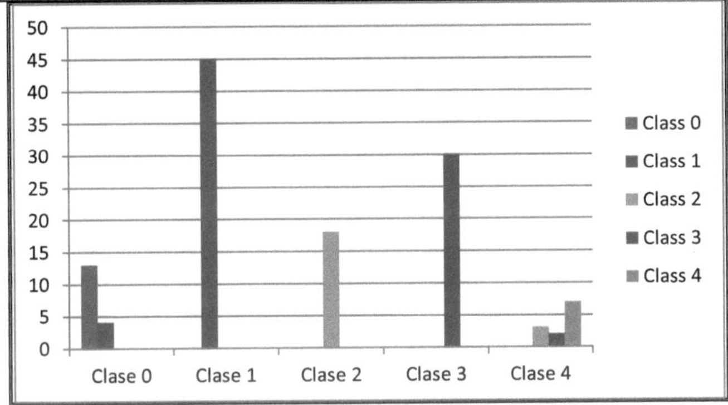

Figure 46Confusion matrix plot.

To obtain the Accuracy which indicates how well trained the model is, the following equation was used:

$$\frac{TP+TN}{(TP+TN+FP+FN)} \qquad (14)$$

This results in an Accuracy of 0.92 which indicates that both in the test and in the training the error is decreasing, indicating that there is no *overfitting*, i.e. in this case the model was well trained and will behave as expected with the new data.

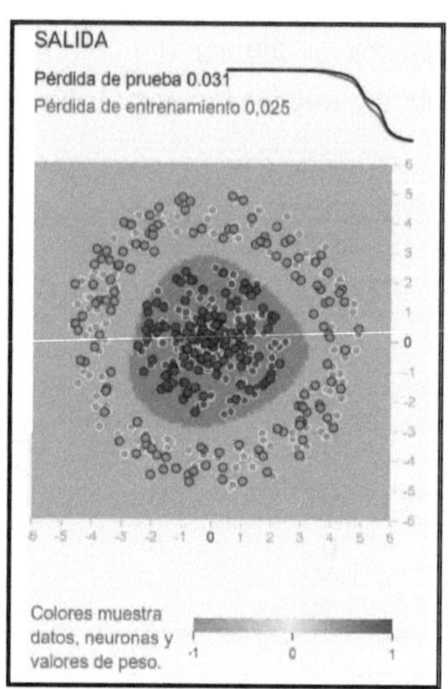

Figure 47Figure: The behaviour of the test error and the training error with quite similar curves where the error decreases.

As can be seen in figure 47, the training and error curves decrease, indicating that there is no overfitting.

It will also show how the prototype performs through the index of sensitivity and accuracy per class.

$$\text{Recall } \frac{TP}{(TP+FN)} \qquad (15)$$

$$\text{Precision } \frac{TP}{(TP+FP)} \qquad (16)$$

Table 7Recall and precision

	Class 0	Class 1	Class 2	Class 3	Class 4	Recall
Class 0		0	0	0	0	1
Class 1		45	0	0	0	0.91
Class 2	0	0		0		0.86
Class 3	0	0	0	30		0.93
Class 4	0	0	0	0		1
Precision	0,76	1	1	1	0.58	0.9

The Accuracy Index indicates how many recognised items are relevant and the Recall indicates how many relevant indices have been selected.

To find a balance between these metrics, the harmonic mean or *F measure* (*F1 score*) is used, the equation for which is shown below:

$$Fmeasure = \frac{TP}{TP+\frac{1}{2}(FP+FN)} \qquad (17)$$

Fmeasure= 0,96

The final evaluation shows Accuracy =0.92 and F measure =0.96.

Both indicators describe a balanced model, which works and will be able to recognise new data and classify them correctly.

Limitations:

In image processing, mathematical models implemented with algorithms in Matlab® were used, and executed with real images (prepared through pre-processing, where noise is eliminated and segmentation is used), which allow the objects of study to be identified, measured and located for classification (defining certain visual characteristics and making use of automatic learning).

It is able to classify with specificity the species presented and at the same time generalise to other species such as bivalves through active thresholds, it does not cause overfitting, but it is limited by the small number of samples, so it is not possible to train in pre-trained Deep Learning models.

Genetic algorithms were also not involved as it was not necessary to achieve an adequate classification.

Discussion:

It was possible to move forward with the presentation of a proposal, which through the use of different methodologies and the incorporation of the transversality property of ICT (Information and Communication Technology), facilitates the performance of human resources in the laboratory, and also manages to automate processes with precision, low equipment cost and short development time. (Information and Communication Technology), facilitates the performance of human resources in the laboratory, and also manages to automate processes with precision, low equipment costs and short development time. Having a laboratory equipped with microscopes and specific filters, the incorporation of a Smartphone does not subtract technology, but rather adds it, as an accessory that offers advantages in the management, acquisition and storage of photographic records.

The application of the prototype achieves self-classification of cell nucleoids for the species under study. Tests have been carried out with images of different species, *Steindachnerina brevipinna (sabalito)*, *Piaractus mesopotamicus* (pacu) and molluscs belonging to the species *Corbicula fluminea* and *Limnoperna fortunei*.

The design of a neuro-fuzzy algorithm manages to differentiate the comet's head, tail and background, distinguishing them in biological material, even in cases where the tail is fuzzy and blurs with the background. It can be analysed to measure and classify them correctly.

Design using computational intelligence allows us to standardise data input through the mathematical algorithms that weight it, reduce the input matrix and optimise training processes, which accelerates learning convergence.

5.2 Proposal to integrate complementary equipment

Some changes or improvements in laboratory equipment would benefit and enable successful implementation. Currently, an epifluorescence microscope is used to analyse cells by EC and a digital camera is used to take the necessary pictures.
- An Olympus CX31 optical microscope, where microphotographs are taken with an Olympus C-5000 ZOOM camera, by means of a tube adapted to the upper part of the microscope to fit the camera.
- A Motic BA310E microscope, which functions as an optical microscope and also has the necessary filters for fluorescence.
As an alternative to the digital cameras described above, AI-ready smartphones (Fig. 47) are proposed that can run applications developed and compiled in Matlab® for example.

This type of AI smartphone processor allows APIs (application programming interface) and frameworks to run on the same phone through its NPU (neural processing unit).

Huawei for example has HIAI mobile computing architecture, a tool for others to develop applications with its mobile AI technology for language recognition, audio analysis, contextual translation, object interpretation through augmented reality, photo interpretation, classification and optimisation, user authentication through pattern recognition and above all very low cost in the market.

Depending on the vectors collected by AI engines, different results will be obtained. As AI developments require power to carry out the calculations, NPUs, GPUs (graphics) and CPUs are used.

The NPU takes care of adjusting this data to realities, applying digital zoom or using its enhanced motion detection system to correct any errors. We can add some microscopy-specific lenses to this mobile phone to allow us to work in greater detail if needed.

In short, as can be seen in Fig. 47, the suggestion is that the prototype presented should be transformed into an application for mobile phones through mobile programming, which would simplify the process of detection, storage, classification and then the counting of cells belonging to each class. With this development, the request to improve the laboratory through the incorporation of Smartphones would be fulfilled.

In the first instance, the mobile phone would replace, at a very low cost, the camera that is currently used, adding improvements such as saving (which allows for a history of samples) and introducing improvements such as applying knowledge management, detection, classification and counting through the execution of the prototype in its cores prepared for this purpose. What these cores or NPUs do is that the APIs and frameworks of the applications that you want to run can do so locally without needing external processors, as applications that do not have this type of technology tend to do. It is also possible to attach specific filters to work with microscopes. These lenses are only attached to the smartphone and a very good performance and photo quality can be obtained. Not only for use in the laboratory but also in the general cytogenetics department, representing a real innovation in the career.

The fact of having this type of device significantly reduces the costs of incorporating technology into the laboratory and increases performance. With the implementation of this type of Smartphone, applications can be developed in the near future to run the prototype presented here, for classification, as can be seen in the diagram presented in Fig. 48.

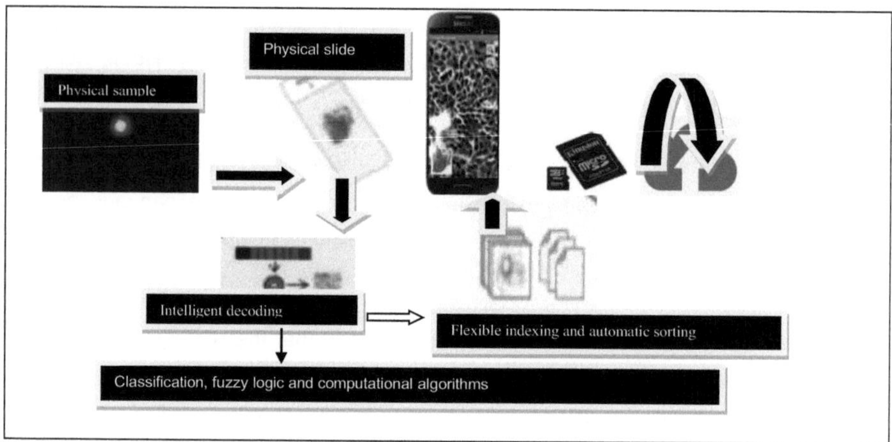

Figure 48Example of the development of the mobile application from the physical sample using the classification prototype and arriving at the intelligent classification of the samples. Own source.

Conclusions

The development and incorporation of new technologies in cytogenetic studies allows another opening to the scientific and technical world, especially in terms of image pattern recognition and computer vision.

This master's thesis not only brings real solutions to the cytogenetics laboratory in its line of research but also in academia where it will become a very useful tool in lectures that include learning the comet assay technique.

In addition, in the professional field, they contribute to the training of human resources specialised in artificial intelligence techniques and their application in image processing.

With respect to the proposed objectives, the self-classification of the images obtained in the 5 classes was obtained using neural networks, neuro-fuzzy algorithms and functions that allow this classification to be carried out automatically with very little margin of error.

The development of the prototypical procedure that classifies the images through the recognition of patterns of cytogenetic images obtained by photography was also achieved. The normalisation or pre-processing was carried out and, as an added value, the creation of the database with the files of the images obtained from the samples when applying the comet test was also generated.

Validation of the prototype was achieved through the case study, with images obtained at the General Cytogenetics and Environmental Monitoring Laboratory of the Institute of Subtropical Biology.

As genuine contributions of this work, we emphasise the reduction in the expert specialist's time, which improves his efficiency. The digital registration of the images also offers the possibility to generate a standard database in such a way that it allows to think about future studies in which historical data are analysed. Compared to some developed software such as "Komet 7" or "Capslab" (mentioned above), as this software was developed specifically for the visual observation method, it improves the time and is extremely useful in the laboratory due to its simplicity. In any case, the photographic sample should be taken as the start of the process, it is simpler as it does not need to be located in the coordinates prepared for each shot, which is required by commercially available software such as Komet7 , and its classification responds to the metrics used in the laboratory. Projections and other types of diagnostics could be achieved in order to prevent endemic diseases, maximising the functionality of early warning signals. In addition, through tools that allow an overview of the management of variables such as key indicators, for example, in dashboards, or through knowledge management or data science.

It also provides an educational and free profile of the development produced in this research, which contributes to the development and preparation of students who learn to classify the cells of different species in a comet test in the Genetics degree programme at the UNAM, the first faculty to incorporate this tool into their training.

After studying different methodologies and carrying out the relevant evaluations, first empirically and then putting various algorithms into practice, it is concluded that neural networks and neuro fuzzy algorithms are an excellent option in the management of cytogenetic images. With this technique, effective optimisation is achieved in the classification of different cell types. Biological characteristics and their natural differences were one of the problems that generated important limitations, given that many models only allowed the classification of *DNA* from a single species. In this study, the model was prepared to classify *DNA* from different species of fish and bivalves with very good results.

A wide variety of Convolutional Neural Network architectures are currently available for free and without usage restrictions, which can achieve reasonable performance in visual recognition tasks. In addition to this, large companies such as Google® or Microsoft® that recognise the importance of data science in our daily activities offer hardware in the Cloud that allows us to use GPUS or TPUS for free without any other requirement for further research.

In the same way, extensive high-level libraries are available, such as KERAS open source, which serves as an abstraction layer on top of Tensor Flow for all kinds of developments. Python, numpy, numba etc. make it relatively easy to train models. Google® also makes available repositories of images and data of all kinds for training and validation of classification and processing algorithms.

This prototype and the experience that comes with the development of different methodologies, algorithms, fusions and applications in a novel hardware with imprints created without limitations, makes it possible to offer data science, artificial intelligence and computer vision in the region.

Our region currently has few exponents in these fields, especially in the field of image pattern recognition. Hence the importance and contribution of this thesis both in the area of BIOTECHNOLOGY as well as in GENETICS.

These first steps encourage to continue developing tools that allow to highlight the training of human resources prepared for technological innovation, from the Master in ICT of the UNaM. It also makes available to society the knowledge or *(know how)* for new developments in different fields, Industrial, Genetic, Biotechnological, Domotics and for the applications of the "Smart City" projects proposed by the province in the development and implementation of the "Knowledge Economies".

As an added value, with the dissemination of these projects through Science Workshops and Congresses, links are established with other Universities that have developments in the area of Data Science or Artificial Intelligence and are interested in working collaboratively expanding our physical limits of Misiones and the NEA to cross borders and integrate knowledge.

Bibliography :

[1]   Flavia Antonela Leveroni, Jacqueline Diana Caffetti, Maria Cristina Pastori, "*Genotoxic response of blood, gill and liver cells of Piaractus mesopotamicus after an acute exposure to a glyphosate-based herbicide,*" Caryologia, 70:1, 21-28, DOI: 10.1080/00087114.2016.1254454.

[2]   S. Wang, D. M. Yang, R. Rong, X. Zhan, and G. Xiao, "*Pathology Image Analysis Using Segmentation Deep Learning Algorithms,*" Am. J. Pathol. vol. 189, n.º 9, pp. 1686-1698, Sep. 2019.

[3]   A. Krizhevsky, I. Sutskever, and G. E. Hinton, "*ImageNet classification with deep convolutional neural networks,*" Commun. ACM, vol. 60, n.º 6, pp. 84-90, 2017.

[4]   H. Takagi and I. Hayashi, "*NN-driven fuzzy reasoning*", Int. J. Approx. Reason. vol. 5, n.º 3, pp. 191-212, 1991.

[5]   C. Quintero, F. Merchán, A. Cornejo, and J. S. Galán, "*Use of Convolutional Neural Networks for Automatic Macroinvertebrate Image Recognition for Participatory Biomonitoring,*" KnE Eng. , vol. 3, n.º 1, p. 585, Feb. 2018.

[6]   D.Sebasti Comas, G.J. Meschino, "*Segmentation of Images through Pattern Recognition*", Esc. y Work. Argenino en Ciencias las Imagenes, 2014.

[7]   A. Bookstein, "*Fuzzy Requests: An Approach to Weighted Boolean Searches*", J. Am. Soc. Inform. Sci. vol. 31, pp. 240-247, 1980.

[8]   Wang Tiesheng and Rao Zhenxing, "*Fuzzy neural network algorithm and its application*", in 2011 International Conference on Electric Technology and Civil Engineering (ICETCE), 2011, pp. 6001-6004.

[9]   Xing, Fuyong,Xie, Yuanpu Su, Hai Liu, Fujun Yang, Lin "*Deep Learning in Microscopy Image Analysis: A Survey*", IEEE Transactions on Neural Networks and Learning Systems. vol 29 1109/TNNLS.2017.2766168.

[10]   M.-Y. Cheng, H.-C. Tsai, C.-H. Ko, and W.-T. Chang, "*Evolutionary Fuzzy Neural Inference System for Decision Making in Geotechnical Engineering,*" J. Comput. Civ. Eng. vol. 22, n.º 4, pp. 272-280, Jul. 2008.

[11]   C. Quintero, F. Merchán, A. Cornejo, and J. S. Galán, "*Use of Convolutional Neural Networks for Automatic Macroinvertebrate Image Recognition for Participatory Biomonitoring,*" KnE Eng. , vol. 3, n.º 1, p. 585, Feb. 2018.

[12]   M. S. Landau and L. Pantanowitz, "*Artificial intelligence in cytopathology: a review of the literature and overview of commercial landscape*", J. Am. Soc. Cytopathol. vol. 8, n.º 4, pp. 230-241, 2019.

[13]   C. Giraldo_Omaira, "*La gestion del conocimiento en las organizaciones y las regiones : una revisión de la literatura the Knowledge Management in the organizatios and the regions* ", n.º 1, 2018.

[14] The MathWorks " *Introducing deep learning with matlab*" Inc. MATLAB and Simulink are registered trademarks of The MathWorks, Inc. 2018.

[15] Colin Walker , "*Ecotoxicology Effects of Pollutants on the Natural Environment* " edit Taylor & Francis Group, an Informa business No claim to original U.S. Government worksVersion Date: 20140513International Standard Book Number-13: 978-1-4822-4700-8 (*eBook* - PDF)

[16]   R. Van der Oost, J. Beyer, and N. P. E. Vermeulen, "*Fish bioaccumulation and biomarkers in environmental risk assessment: A review*", Environmental Toxicology and Pharmacology, vol. 13, n.º 2. pp. 57-149, Feb-2003.

[17] O. Ostling and K. J. Johanson, "*Microelectrophoretic study of radiation-induced DNA damages in individual mammalian cells*", Biochem. Biophys. Res. Commun. vol. 123, n.º 1, pp. 291-298, Aug. 1984.

[18] N. Singh, MT. McCoy, R. Tice EL Schneider "*A simple technique for quantitation of low levels of DNA damage in individual cells*". Exp Cell Res. 1988;175(1):184-191. doi:10.1016/0014-4827(88)90265-0

[19] *J. D. Caffetti, M S. Mantovani, M. C. Pastori and A S. Fenocchio " First genotoxicity study of Paraná river water from Argentina using cells from the clam Corbicula fluminea (Veneroida Corbiculidae) and Chinesehamster (Cricetulus griseus Rodentia, Cricetidae) K1 cells in the comet assay" Genetics and Molecular Biology, 31, 2, 561-565 (2008).*
Sociedade Brasileira de Genética, Brazil.

[20] M. MN Authman, MS Zaki, EA Khallaf, H. Abbas "*Use of Fish as Bio-indicator of the Effects of Heavy Metals Pollution*". Hydrobiology Department, National Research Centre, 33 EL Bohouth St. (Former EL Tahrir St.), Dokki, Giza, Egypt, Faculty of Science, Minufiya University, Shebeen Alkoom, Egypt Authman et al., J Aquac Res Development 2015, 6:4 DOI: 10.4172/2155-9546.1000328

[21] A. P. Boyle, J. Guinney, G. E. Crawford, and T. S. Furey, "*F-Seq: A feature density estimator for high-throughput sequence tags*", Bioinformatics, vol. 24, n.º 21, pp. 2537-2538, Nov. 2008.

[22] A. M.Gonzalez, J. L.Gonzalez C. B. Loeza, A. Espinosa, Pacheco-Pantoja "*Introduction to Cell Segmentation Techniques of the Comet Assay* "Ingeniería Revista Académica de la Facultad de Ingeniería Universidad Autónoma de Yucatán". vo 22 Num 3(2018) . ISSN: 2448-8364.

[23] F. Neri and V. Tirronen, "*Scale factor local search in differential evolution*", *Memetic Comput.* Jun. 2009, vol. 1, n.º 2, pp. 153-171.

[24] C. Quintero, F. Merchán, A. Cornejo, and J. S. Galán, "*Use of Convolutional Neural Networks for Automatic Macroinvertebrate Image Recognition for Participatory Biomonitoring," KnE Eng.* , vol. 3, n.º 1, p. 585, Feb. 2018.

[25] LeCun, L Bottou, Y Bengio, and P Haffner. "*Gradient-based learning applied to document recognition*". Proceedings of the IEEE, (1998). 86 (11), 2278-2324.

[26] Krizhevsky, A., Sutskever, I. and Hinton, GE "*Imagenet classification with deep convolutional neural networks*". In Advances in neural information processing systems(2012). (pp. 1097-1105).

[27] Szegedy, C., Liu, W., Jia, Y., Sermanet, P., Reed, S., Anguelov, D., Rabinovich, A. "*Deepening convolutions".* In Proceedings of the IEEE (2015) Conference on Computer Vision and Pattern Recognition (pp. 1-9).

[28] K. C. Chang, Y. W. Chiang, C. H. Yang, and J. W. Liou, "*Atomic force microscopy in biology and biomedicine," Tzu Chi Medical Journal.* Buddhist Compassion Relief Tzu Chi Foundation. Published by Elsevier Taiwan LLC. All rights reserved. July 2012

[29] S. Robertson, H. Azizpour, K. Smith, and J. Hartman, "*Digital image analysis in breast pathology-from image processing techniques to artificial intelligence*", *Transl. Res.* vol. 194, pp. 19-35, 2018.

[30] S. K. Oh, W. Pedrycz, and B. J. Park, "*Self-organizing neurofuzzy networks based on evolutionary fuzzy granulation", IEEE Trans. Syst. Man, Cybern. Part ASystems Humans.* vol. 33, n.º 2, pp. 271-277, Mar. 2003.

[31] J. C. F. Silva, R. M. Teixeira, F. F. Silva, S. H. Brommonschenkel, and E. P. B. Fontes, "Machine learning approaches and their current application in plant

molecular biology: systematic review," Plant Sci.   P. B. Fontes, "*Machine learning approaches and their current application in plant molecular biology: A systematic review*", *Plant Sci.* vol. 284, pp. 37-47, 2019.

[32] M. K. K. K. Niazi, A. V Parwani, and M. N. Gurcan, "*Digital pathology and artificial intelligence*," *Lancet Oncol.* , vol. 20, n.º 5, pp. e253-e261, May 2019.

[33] V. M. Garcia Luna, "*Introduction to digital signal processing*", *Elai-Upm*, vol. 1, p. 5, 2001.

[34] M. Mart, "*Classical Image Segmentation Techniques*", *Ecologia*, n.º 1, pp. 1-23, 2004.

[35] K. J. Lee and H. P. Soyer, "*Smartphones, artificial intelligence and digital histopathology take on basal cell carcinoma diagnosis,*" *Br. J. Dermatol.* , p. bjd.18374, Aug. 2019.

[36] M. Gamarra, F. Bertel, J. Velasquez "*Software Tool for Learning Fuzzy Systems in a Digital Control Course*". Form. Univ. La Serena 2016, vol.9, n.4 pp.33-40. ISSN 0718-5006.

[37] H. Takagi, N. Suzuki, T. Koda, and Y. Kojima, "*Neural networks designed on approximate reasoning architecture and their applications*", *IEEE Trans. Neural Networks*, vol. 3, n.º 5, pp. 752-760, 1992.

[38] F. Yin, J. Jun L. J. Wang, C. Guo, Dalian li gong da xue, Chinese University of Hong Kong, and IEEE Circuits and Systems Society, "*Advances in neural networks*" ISNN 2004 : International Symposium on Neural Networks, Dalian, China, August 19-21, 2004 : proceedings. Springer, 2004.

[39] *Horzyk A., Tadeusiewicz R.* "Self-Optimizing *Neural Networks*". In: Yin FL., Wang J., Guo C. (eds) Advances in Neural Networks - ISBN 978-3-540-22841-7 Lecture Notes in Computer Science, vol 3173. Springer, Berlin, HeidelbergA. icz, , pp. 150-155.

[40] Rodriguez,AC "Reticularism or neuronism: Different perception of the same circumstance" Archives of neuroscience(MexicoDF). vol 10 n1 (print version ISSN0187-4705 2005].

[41] N. Kalchbrenner, E. Grefenstette, and P. Blunsom, "A convolutional neural network for modelling sentences," in *52nd Annual Meeting of the Association for Computational Linguistics, ACL 2014 - Proceedings of the Conference*, 2014, vol. 1, pp. 655-665.

[42] S. Apu and S. Apu, "Hypertrophy", in *ECG for Medical Diagnosis*, vol. 10, n.º 1, Jaypee Brothers Medical Publishers (P) Ltd., 2018, pp. 63-63.

[43] Thamer M.Jamel, B.M.K., " Implementation of a sigmoid activation function for neural network using FPGA". 13th Scientific I Published in the 13th Scientific Conference of Al-Ma'moon University College -18 April 2012 - Baghdad , Iraq .

[44] Ramirez Q. Juan A. and Chacon M. Mario I. " Artificial neural networks for image processing, a review of the last decade " RIEE&C, Journal of electronic and computer engineering, Vol. 9 No. 1, July 2011. ISSN 1870 - 9532

[45] Du, Zhenlong, Li, Xiaoli "Laplacian filtering effect on digital image tuning via the decomposed eigen-filter" Computers and Electrical Engineering vol 78 (print version) ISSN 00457906.

[46] Rojas, T., Sanz, W., and Arteaga F.(2008). "Computer vision system for the detection of spherical objects through the Hough transform". Revista Ingeniería UC, 15 (1), 77-87.

[47] Perez-Teruel, Karina; Leyva-Vazquez, Maikel; Espinilla, Macarena and Estrada-Senti, Vivian. "Computation with words in decision making using fuzzy

cognitive maps". Rev cuba cienc informat 2014, vol.8, n.2, pp.19-34. ISSN 2227-1899.

[48] Sutton , Richard S, Barto, Andrew G "Reinforcement Learning"(Machine learning. Series Q325.6.S88 1998.Kindle edition.ISBN 0-262-19398-1.

[49] Goodfellow, Ian, Bengio, Yoshua and Courville, Aaron. (2016, December). "MIT Press ISBN-13: 978-0262035613.

[50] Vera Laceiras M.S, Caffetti Y. "Pattern recognition of digital images obtained by microscopy and parameterized according to the Micronucleus technique and the Comet Assay Technique used by the Laboratory of General Cytogenetics and Environmental Monitoring UNaM-IBS CONICET for the detection of cell damage". Ctes. 2018 Red UNCI - UNNE - ISBN 978-987-3619-27-4 Editorial Universidad Nacional del Nordeste (UNNE) 2018. Red de Universidades con Carreras en Informática (RedUNCI). http://sedici.unlp.edu.ar/handle/10915/692053

[51] Vera Laceiras M. Silvia and Caffetti Yanina; "Pattern recognition of digital images obtained by microscopy and parameterized according to the Micronucleus technique and the Comet Assay Technique used by the Laboratory of General Cytogenetics and Environmental Monitoring UNaM-IBS CONICET for the detection of cell damage". Encarnación-Paraguay 2019 SAETA Academic and scientific university of the documentation centre of the Univ. Autónoma de EncarnaciónISSN: 2414 2506. https://www.unae.edu.py/tv/images/Memoria-del-I-Congreso-Internacional-de-ciencia-diseno-tecnologia-UNAE-2019.pdf3

[52] Vera Laceiras M. Silvia; "Digital processing of cytogenetic images for classification according to the comet assay technique for the detection of DNA damage". Calafate 2020 (UNCI Network) - article 12770 belonging to the area "Intelligent Agents and Systems". https://wicc2020.unpa.edu.ar/ WICC 2020 (Workshop on Computer Science developed virtually by the pandemic).

yes I want morebooks!

Buy your books fast and straightforward online - at one of world's fastest growing online book stores! Environmentally sound due to Print-on-Demand technologies.

Buy your books online at
www.morebooks.shop

Kaufen Sie Ihre Bücher schnell und unkompliziert online – auf einer der am schnellsten wachsenden Buchhandelsplattformen weltweit! Dank Print-On-Demand umwelt- und ressourcenschonend produziert.

Bücher schneller online kaufen
www.morebooks.shop

info@omniscriptum.com
www.omniscriptum.com